MINNE

ON-THE-ROAD HISTORIES

MINNESOTA

John Radzilowski

Interlink Books

*To Joseph Amato, who taught me to look at the place
where I lived*

First published in 2006 by

INTERLINK BOOKS
An imprint of Interlink Publishing Group, Inc.
46 Crosby Street, Northampton, Massachusetts 01060
www.interlinkbooks.com

Library of Congress Cataloging-in-Publication Data
Radzilowski, John, 1965–
Minnesota/John Radzilowski
p. cm. — (On-the-road histories)
Includes bibliographical references.
ISBN 1-56656-567-7 (pbk.)
1. Minnesota—History. 2. Minnesota—Description and
travel. 3. Minnesota—History, Local. I. Title. II. Series.
F606.R33 2004
977.6—dc22   2004022154

*Black and white historical images are courtesy of the
Minnesota Historical Society; Color images © Steve Skjold
Photography*

Printed in China

*Left: Flowers surround a stop sign in Edina
Below: Paddleboat and sailboat on the Mississippi River, St. Paul*

CONTENTS

IX. New Places, New Faces 199

Minnesota Liberalism—Suburbanization
Newcomers—The Loss of the Small Towns

INTRODUCTION

What the heck is Minnesota? Who the heck are Minnesotans? As the old travel guides used to say, "Minnesota is a land of contrasts."

Look at a map of North America without the handy national and state borders and try to locate Minnesota. Lake Superior is easy enough to find, as is the Red River along Minnesota's northwestern border, and the Mississippi, which forms part of the state's southeastern border. But to the southwest, north, and south, the boundaries are not as clear. Minnesota is a place whose contours are only partly defined by landscape.

Minnesota is many landscapes, but none of them fully defines her. Michigan is a Great Lakes state, shaped and formed by North America's freshwater inland seas. Nebraska is a Great Plains state, Idaho a Rocky Mountain state. But of what great geographic feature is Minnesota a part? And what region is it in? Is Minnesota a midwestern state? Once it was called a northwestern state. Easterners see it as part of the west; Westerners as part of the east. Minnesotans often split the difference and call their home "the Upper Midwest."

Everyone, save Canadians, agrees that it is in the north.

Within Minnesota's boundaries fall parts of several landscapes and major geographical features. So take your pick.

In the north, Minnesota borders Lake Superior, the greatest of the continent's inland seas, sharing part of the Great Lakes. The western third of the state formed part of the tall-grass prairie, the eastern edge of the range of the great buffalo herds and the horse culture of the native peoples of the Great Plains. Central and Southeast Minnesota were once the far western fringe of the great deciduous woodlands that filled most of the eastern half of the continent prior to European arrival. In the north are bogs, lakes, and pine forests, the southern end of a forest range stretching all the way to the Canadian sub arctic.

Its rivers are no less diverse. The St. Louis River runs east to Lake Superior. The waters of the Rainy and Red Rivers go north to Lake Winnipeg and eventually reach Hudson's Bay. The Mississippi and its tributaries, the St. Croix, Minnesota, and Des Moines flow south to the Gulf of Mexico.

Minnesota's shape is a function of its political boundaries and of the homes people made within those boundaries over time. Yet for all that, Minnesotans know who they are by where they are. In as much as it is defined by anything, Minnesotan identity is defined by a strong identification with place, be it an urban neighborhood, a farmstead with its attendant shelter-belt "grove," or the familiar water tower and church steeples that mark the skyline of one the state's small towns.

It is not enough to be merely from Minnesota, but from a place. Although the Twin Cities border each other, they are in some sense different worlds. Wags often assert with some truth that Minneapolis people rarely venture into St. Paul and vice versa. Within the metro area, there are neighborhoods—such as "Nordeast" Minneapolis, Rondo, the east side of St. Paul, or West St. Paul—that have distinct identities based on ethnicity, religion, and class that have remained intact even when many of the old residents have moved to the suburbs. "Outstate" Minnesota, that part of the state beyond the sprawling metro area—what one governor proudly declared "Greater Minnesota"—defines itself negatively, as not being part of the Twin Cities area. So, too, with the small towns. There is no "Lake Wobegon" homogeneity here: New Ulm is a German town, Alexandria Norwegian, Chisago City Swedish, Little Canada French Canadian, Sobieski Polish, Ghent Belgian, Minneota Icelandic, and so on.

The best known Minnesota identity comes from the Range, that is, the Iron Range of northeast Minnesota, whose people were shaped by the state's great iron mines from a proud mix of primarily Finnish and eastern and southern European immigrants. Even as the mines have closed, the "Rangers" have maintained their identity through Iron Range clubs, some as far afield as Manhattan, where they might follow the hockey team once known as the Eveleth Rangers, but more recently renamed for New York.

Winter used to be a defining characteristic of the state, a perverse point of pride for natives. The wind-chill factor made Minnesotans hearty, and the stories of digging tunnels to get out of your house after some legendary blizzard always guaranteed looks of amazement from visitors from the southern states. Since the advent of Sunbelt retirement communities, urbanization, imported TV news anchors, and indoor football, however, Minnesotans have grown more allergic to the cold. Still, most Minnesotans know that an ice house is not a place to store ice but a place to bond with friends and family and perhaps catch some fish while perched on a frozen lake.

Long after racial and ethnic attributes fell out of fashion, Minnesotans and non-Minnesotans alike often ascribed the state's unique characteristics to its "Nordic" ethnic "stock." (Even today, visitors will express surprise to discover long-standing communities of African Americans, Latinos, Poles, Jews, or Italians in the supposedly all Scandinavian state.) Those unique characteristics include a liberal or "progressive" political tradition—with all its alleged connotations of goodness—as well as a clean environment, tolerance, and good government and schools.

Minnesotans, too, buy into the myth for better or worse. The state consistently places near the top of indicators for quality of life, economic well-being, health, and education. Rochester, with the famous Mayo Clinic and a high proportion of doctors, ranks among America's most liveable small cities. Minnesotans have a good state and most of them realize it.

And then there is "Minnesota Nice," that elusive characteristic that is neither gracious Southern hospitality nor hearty back-slapping but rather a kind of polite caring that means to be helpful but not too intrusive. Of course, at times Minnesota Nice seems to be merely Minnesota Smug, but not too often.

Poised between both coasts, Minnesota is fly-over country to some, God's country to others, and Minnesotans are of two minds, feeling both superior for what the state has and inferior for the ways it is not New York or Los Angeles. Within the same conversation Minnesotans can deplore their state's backwardness compared to the big cultural, economic, and media centers of America while also expressing pride. As Minnesotans like to say in their understated way, the state is "a pretty good place."

In the Paleozoic era (about 600 to 300 million years ago), warm seas covered parts of the state. They disappeared but were replaced with another ocean about 100 million years ago, which was home to ancient sharks, reptiles, and invertebrates. This body of water, too, dried or drained away, leaving behind only the fossil remains of its inhabitants.

Approximately two million years ago, great ice sheets began to creep southward over the state, covering it in whole or part in four successive waves, with the last invasion ending a mere 12,000 years ago. Evidence of their passage is everywhere in Minnesota, from deep grooves carved in old granite and fields strewn with boulders to high glacial moraines and rich soils.

As the final ice invasion began to retreat, the melting glaciers created a giant lake, Lake Agassiz, which covered northwest Minnesota, western Ontario, and much of southern Manitoba and Saskatchewan. Shallow, but larger in surface area than all five of today's Great Lakes combined, Lake Agassiz waxed and waned. At its height about 12,000 years ago, the lake waters rose high enough to

Winter at the north shore of Lake Superior

break through the continental divide and rush southward, carving the giant channel of the Minnesota River valley.

THE LAND AND WATER

In 1836 the renowned artist George Catlin marveled at the glaciers' work on Minnesota:

> I believe that the geologist may take the varieties which he may gather… in one hour and travel the continent of North America all over without being able to put them all in place; coming at last to the unavoidable conclusion that numerous chains or beds of primitive rocks have reared their heads on this continent, the summits of which have been swept away by the force of diluvial currents; and their fragments jostled together and strewed about like foreigners in a strange land, over the great valleys of the Mississippi and Missouri, where they will ever remain and gazed on by the traveler as the only remaining evidence of their native ledges.

Must-See Sites: Jeffers Petroglyphs, Jeffers

Amid the prairie grasses are islands of uncovered rock where the first Minnesotans left carvings of humans, deer, elk, buffalo, turtles, thunderbirds, atlatls, and arrows. One of the Upper Midwest best-known prehistoric sites tells a story that spans 5,000 years. The glyphs, which range in date from 3000 BCE to 1750 CE, served many functions, including recording important events, depicting sacred ceremonies, and emphasizing the importance of animals and hunting. Here, visitors can catch a glimpse of the life and culture of the region's first inhabitants. A new visitor center with exhibits, a multimedia pre-sentation, rest-rooms, and drinking fountains, is now open.

Contact: (507) 628-5591; E-mail: jefferspetroglyphs@mnhs.org; Web: www.mnhs.org

Location: Near Comfrey and Windom, three miles east of U.S. Hwy 71 on Cottonwood County Road 10, then one mile south on County Road 2.

As the glaciers gradually receded, they left behind thousands of depressions carved out of the land that filled with water to become Minnesota's famous lakes. After the glaciers came tundra and following the tundra were forests of pine, birch, ash, and spruce. Along with this change came numerous species of early mammals and on their heels the region's first Native Americans. About 8,000 years ago, a warm, dry period in earth's history caused the forests to die out, replaced instead by broad grasslands with small stands of trees. Beginning roughly 4,000 years ago, the climate again became cooler and wetter, and forests returned across much of Minnesota, creating the landscape seen by the first European explorers.

Its lakes notwith-standing, the state's climate is continental and more than once compared to Siberia. The winters are cold, the summers hot and often humid. Minnesota has pro-verbially harsh winters. Although the myth is often greater than the reality, International Falls in far northern Minnesota holds the title of the "the Nation's Icebox," and the state itself holds records for the lowest temperatures in the lower 48 states. Precipitation is variable, with the western third of the state receiving 16–24 inches annually and the rest 24–40 inches.

Minnesota is a land of water. In western Minnesota, lower rainfall amounts and small, shallow lakes and sloughs characterize the tall-grass prairie. In eastern and central Minnesota, the Mississippi and tributaries mark a region of deciduous forest. In the north and northeast, wetlands, peat bogs, rivers, and lakes make the north country a land of coniferous forest. Water also drives human history, providing resources that sustained the native peoples and highways for fur traders and later shippers of grain, ore, and timber. Water drained from prairie wetlands created some of the world's most productive agriculture. Lakes shaped Minnesota's tourist industry, which began within a few decades of statehood. And while water gives, it also takes, in the form of recurring cycles of drought and flood.

Lakes give the state its proudest title and are its best-known water resources. Lake Superior, shared with Wisconsin, Michigan, and Ontario, is the largest body of fresh water in the world. Over 1,300 feet deep, Superior is an inland sea. Even in the height of summer it remains so cold as to be barely swimable. In the fall, its violent storms have destroyed the largest and most advanced ships, while in winter it is completely icebound. Two of the state's other major lakes, Lake of the Woods and Rainy Lake, line its border with Canada, while wholly within Minnesota's borders lie Upper and Lower Red Lake, Lake Mille Lacs, and Leech Lake, to name only the largest bodies. Yet for most Minnesotans, who each summer spend time "up at the lake," the "lake" means one of the state's many smaller and more intimately knowable bodies, with cabins, trees, boat launches, and swimming beaches. Even the state's largest cities have sizable lakes within their limits or nearby. The western side of the metro area has its lakes Harriet, Nokomis, and Minnetonka, while the eastern side has its lakes Como and Phalen.

In addition to lakes and rivers, Minnesota has other abundant wetlands, be they marshes, peat bogs, or prairie sloughs. These areas function as habitats for a wide variety of wildlife, including the infamous Minnesota mosquito, jokingly referred to as the state bird. The wetlands also filter and retain runoff from heavy rains. In agricultural and urban areas, the demand for land has led to the draining of many wetlands and sloughs (shallow, seasonal lakes or marshes), greatly complicating water management.

Natural Regions

Minnesota's waters are a common element of the state's three main natural regions: the North Country, with its pine forests, lakes, and bogs; the tall-grass prairie, the eastern part of the Great Plains; and the Upper Mississippi valley, with its mix of deciduous forests and prairies. When European explorers first set eyes on the region and when American settlers came to live here, they imagined that the state's landscape and nature had existed as it was from time immemorial. After all "nature" implied the absence of human beings. In reality, however, long before the arrival of Europeans, Minnesota's native peoples had been gradually shaping and changing the landscape to suit their purposes. Since then, the descendents of the European settlers and immigrants have engaged in much of the same endeavor, albeit with greater power and different technology. In both cases, the results can be viewed as a mixed bag. Nevertheless, Minnesota's landscape is the result of human action as well as the forces of climate, water, and ecology.

The Upper Mississippi Valley region of Minnesota is the western edge of the great eastern woodland, a swath of deciduous forest and mixed forest-prairie that once covered much of the eastern United States and the southern Great Lakes. In Minnesota, this ecological area covers the state in a belt paralleling the course of the Mississippi from the Iowa border to Brainerd and Detroit Lakes, including the southeastern corner of the state and the Twin Cities metro area, the St. Croix valley, and lower stretches of the Minnesota River north of Mankato.

The wooded eastern landscape, called the Big Woods by early settlers, has a mixed ecological face. There are river bottoms, upland forests, and small patches of prairie, as well as different distributions of dominant tree types, each forming unique habitats. Maple, basswood, and oak are predominate in many areas, providing spectacular fall leaf shows, while stands of the prolific sugar maple, called sugar bushes, have provided the makings of maple syrup for centuries. Forest floors are often free of shrubs, except where an older tree has fallen, letting sunlight filter in. Interspersed

Must-See Sites: Itasca State Park, Park Rapids

Established in 1891, Itasca is Minnesota's oldest state park and the site of the headwaters of America's greatest river, the Mississippi. The park totals more than 32,000 acres and includes more than 100 lakes. Walk across the mighty Mississippi as it starts its winding journey 2,552 miles to the Gulf of Mexico. Stand under towering pines at Preacher's Grove. Visit the Itasca Indian Cemetery or Wegmann's Cabin, landmarks of centuries gone by. Camp under the stars, or stay the night at the historic Douglas Lodge or cabins. Explore Wilderness Drive past the 2,000-acre Wilderness Sanctuary, one of Minnesota's seven National Natural Landmarks. The diverse vegetation in the park supports many wildlife species. Birding is excellent and visitors are encouraged to help spot and record the bird life they see in the park. Some birds you can expect to see include loons, grebes, cormorants, herons, ducks, owls, hummingbirds, woodpeckers, chickadees, nuthatches, kinglets, vireos, tanagers, finches, and warblers. Trails in the park are shared with deer, chipmunks, and squirrels. Beaver, porcupine, black bears, and wolves also reside in the park.

The park itself has been inhabited for some 8,000 years, from the time when Native American hunters pursued wild animals for food in the Itasca State Park region. These early people ambushed bison, deer, and moose at watering sites and killed them with stone-tipped spears. The Bison Kill site along Wilderness Drive in the park gives visitors more history about this period. A few thousand years later, a group of people of the Woodland Period arrived at Lake Itasca. They lived in larger, more permanent settlements and made a variety of stone, wood, and bone tools. Burial mounds from this era can be seen today at the Itasca Indian Cemetery. In 1832, Anishinabe guide Ozawindib led explorer Henry Rowe Schoolcraft to the source of the Mississippi River at Lake Itasca.

Contact: E-mail: itasca.park@dnr.state.mn.us; Web: www.dnr.state.mn.us/state_parks/ or www.stayatmnparks.com

Location: Entrance to the park is 21 miles north of Park Rapids on U.S. Highway 71. From Bemidji the park is 30 miles south on U.S. Hwy 71.

with the forests are upland clearings (called prairies by early French explorers), formed most likely by early Native Americans' use of fire. The burning created open areas that were welcoming to small herds of grazing animals, such as buffalo and elk that in turn provided good hunting. When the Europeans arrived, they found a land that had been shaped by human habitation. As geographer John Hudson noted: "Whether prairies for grazing or bottomlands for corn, these lands required as little work to bring them into bumper-crop production as any encountered in the course of westward expansion in the United States."

These eastern forests support a variety of wildlife, including herbivores such as deer, woodchucks, squirrels, and cottontail rabbits; omnivores such as black bear, raccoon, and skunk; and in former times predators such as the timber wolf. Streams and wetlands were also home to beaver and muskrat. Wild turkey, herons, woodpeckers, a plethora of songbirds, and in past times the now-extinct passenger pigeon filled the air with song and the beating of wings.

The Mississippi River basin defines Minnesota's eastern woodland. The thickest belts of deciduous forest covered its water course and surrounding lands. Over the centuries, as the river changed course it carved new channels and river beds, leaving behind floodplains that became prime habitat for elm, silver maple, cottonwood, and willow, as well as home to large colonies of beaver.

Covering roughly the western third of the state, including all of southwestern and west-central Minnesota as well as much of the broad, flat valley of the Red River, the Land of the Tall Grass is Minnesota's claim to being the gateway to the west. Beyond are the Dakotas, the High Plains, and the Rocky Mountains. Although today 99 percent of the former prairie ecosystem has been replaced by production agriculture, the lay of the land is essentially unchanged. Distant horizons and big skies remain. For many travelers used to more intimate landscapes, the plains can be psychologically daunting. Washington Irving wrote in 1835 that "here we have an immense extent of landscape without a sign of human existence. We have the consciousness of being far, far beyond the bounds of human habitation; we feel as if moving into a desert world."

Mississippi River, St. Paul

Many observers here feel they are always in the center of the landscape, always perfectly placed equidistant from all horizons. Minnesota author Paul Gruchow wrote:

> I cannot explain why this landscape seems so flat.... It is flat, I suppose, as the deserts are flat, as the oceans are flat, as the polar ice caps are flat. It is flat because of the immensity of its distances.... What is flat seems empty. When we are faced with vastness on the scale of the prairie, we turn inward.... The prairie is like a daydream. It is one of those plainly visible things you cannot photograph. No camera lens can take in a big enough piece of it.... The experience is a kind of baptism. To live on the prairie is to daydream. It is the only conceivable response to such an immensity. It is when we are smallest that our daydreams come quickest.

Yet the prairie is never perfectly flat, even in the Red River Valley. There are gently undulating hills, small streams and rivers, and the occasional prairie lake. Along the Minnesota–South Dakota border, the Coteau des Prairie, also called Buffalo Ridge, rises up, a moraine formed by glacial action. From the top of the moraine to the regional center of Marshall, a distance of 40 miles, the little Redwood River descends 635 feet, a distance greater than the Mississippi falls between St. Paul and New Orleans.

The prairie was the kingdom of grass and herbs: switchgrass, bluestem, heath aster, compass plant, Indian grass, porcupine grass, and prairie dropseed. It grew so high that in mid summer it could hide a horse and rider. In the spring, hundreds of tiny flowers would carpet the ground, especially around wetlands. The grass created a thick layer of sod rich in nutrients that provided sustenance for birds, gophers and mice, which in turn provided food for badgers and hawks.

Like the Big Woods, the prairie was the product of human, climate, and animal interactions. Frequent burning by native people cut back woody plants and encouraged the growth of herds of buffalo. Early travelers in western Minnesota commonly reported herds numbering in the thousands (though even larger herds were found further west).

Hundreds of wetlands and shallow lakes, providing seasonal habitat for migrating waterfowl, also dotted the prairie. There, and in river bottoms, stands of trees grew up, protected from natural and man-made fires. The wetlands ranged from seasonal sloughs or marshes, to potholes carved by the glaciers, to full-fledged lakes. One of the latter was the Great Oasis in Murray County, a group of four interconnected bodies of water. Local residents remember that the woods around the Oasis were "a haven for berrypickers who found wild raspberries, goose-berries, currants, choke-cherries, plums, and grapes. In the spring, white trillium and Dutch-man's breeches bloomed on the forest floor as well as Canadian wild ginger, bloodroot, and jack-in-the-pulpit. Birds were profuse." Like so many of the prairie wetlands, however, the Great Oasis was drained for crop land. As a local newspaper reporter put it in 1913: "Hardly a drop [of] water remains in Bear Lake. A little water remains in the ditch here and there, but the bulk of the water is gone and the hunter bloweth his duck call in vain for the ducks that are not."

Famous Minnesotans: Bob Dylan

Born Robert Allen Zimmerman, Duluth, May 24, 1941.

One of the most influential figures in American popular music, Bob Dylan was born Robert Zimmerman, the son of a Hibbing merchant. He grew up in northern Minnesota and attended college at the University of Minnesota in Minneapolis. Throughout these early years, Dylan absorbed many musical influences, especially folk, country, blues, and early rock 'n' roll. By 1960, he had changed his name and begun performing in beatnik coffee houses. He developed as a performer, honing his unique, spare lyrical style. After moving to New York in 1961, he had a major impact on the folk music scene in Greenwich Village. He signed his first record deal with Columbia in 1961. The following year, he wrote "Blowin' in the Wind," which became a major anthem of the era and brought him national attention. Many believe Dylan's best years as a songwriter were 1964–66. By then he had begun experimenting with electronic music and new styles. Dylan has continued to put out albums and perform to large audiences and received nearly every honor and acclaim possible in popular music. He has been described as one of the greatest musical poets of the late twentieth century.

The North Country is a land of coniferous forests, lakes, and peat bogs that constitutes the northeastern third of the state, from the Arrowhead and North Shore of Lake Superior, Duluth, the Iron Range, and west to Red Lake and north to Ontario. It suffered extensive logging in the nineteenth and early twentieth centuries, and today's forest is usually second growth. Parts of it, however, especially along the Boundary Waters, retain much of its primeval feel. Charles Ira Cook, who trapped in the Boundary Waters in the early 1920s, recalled:

> The whole universe, as we surveyed it, was alive. Birds called from the shore, fish leaped or left concentric rings on the surface as they broke the water in feeding. Far down the lake a loon pierced the stillness with its chilly, vacant laugh…. On this, the first of the lakes we were to travel, we saw our first deer. He came tumbling out of the brush and spilled into the water just ahead of us as though startled by some unseen marauder in the darkness of the thicket. Striking out majestically, he crossed in front of our canoe in great surges, so close that we could see little beads of water clinging to the velvet of his young horns like pearls on the plush mat of a jeweler's counter.

At the time of European exploration, northern Minnesota was covered with great forests of white and red pine, white cedar, and other species. These old-growth forests benefited from the occasional forest fire, which helped prune back dead wood and underbrush and make way for young trees. A great diversity of wildlife thrived in these forest: beaver, woodland caribou, moose, deer, wolves, coyotes, porcupines, martens, weasels, bear, otter, bald eagles, and even mountain lion. Of these, the caribou and mountain lion are mostly gone, although an occasional lion sighting is not unknown. Wolves were hunted out of the state by the early twentieth century but have been reintroduced to northern Minnesota in recent times.

Although heavily used for logging, mining, and recreation, Minnesota's northern forest regions remain the least populated and most mythologized. Most Minnesotans retain an image of the north country in their consciousness, as shown by recent choices for sports teams like the

Must-See Sites: International Wolf Center, Ely

The International Wolf Center, the world's premier wolf interpretive facility, sits in the heart of the Superior National Forest in Ely, gateway to the Boundary Waters Canoe Area. Since humans first drew petroglyphs to record their observations, wolves have populated the art, literature, and culture of our planet. The howl of the wolf sends shivers of fascination and love, or fear and distrust, up the backs of people around the world. Hardly anyone treats the wolf with indifference. This non-profit research center is devoted to the study of the wolf and has been instrumental to the wolf's successful reintroduction to northern Minnesota. The center's flagship facility features triangular windows designed to represent wolf eyes and ears. The observation windows look into a 1.25-acre wolf enclosure and den site that is home for the resident wolf pack. Born in April 1993, three wolves serve as ambassadors for the educational mission of the International Wolf Center. The center's Ely facility offers a variety of educational programs for adults and families. Afternoon, weekend and weeklong visits include howling trips, radio tracking, snowshoe treks, family activities, dogsledding, videos, presentations, flights over wolf country, demonstrations, and hikes. Programs are custom designed for groups of all ages.

Contact: (218) 365-4695; Web: www.wolf.org
Location: On Highway 169 near Ely.

Timberwolves and the Wild. Pictures of Lake Superior's North Shore, with its craggy rock formations, lighthouses, and wild expanses of woods and water are stock in trade for promoters of Minnesota tourism. Although today, Minnesotans are overwhelmingly and increasingly urban and their state is tamed and pasturized, the idea of Minnesota as a big and wild land with wide prairies, deep forests, and glassy lakes punctuated by a loon's haunting cry are part of a mental landscape that has defined the state and its people and continues to do so.

2

THE FIRST MINNESOTANS

People have lived in Minnesota for a very long time. They have been here since the glaciers retreated, glacial lakes such as Agassiz expanded, and the Minnesota River valley was carved by run-off. As grass and trees colonized the land in the glacier's wake, they were followed by prehistoric animals, including mastodon and giant beaver, as well as the more common deer, elk, and bison. These in turn were followed by groups of people, the region's first Native Americans.

Evidence in the form of Clovis-style spearpoints, scattered though it may be, indicates a human presence in southern and southwestern Minnesota perhaps as early as 9500 BCE, or more than 11,000 years ago. At Browns Valley, near the Minnesota–South Dakota border, human remains found in the 1930s have since been reliably dated at 9,000 years old. Prior to about 6000 BCE (what archaeologists term the Paleoindian period) humans were few in number in Minnesota, and they left behind only some small caches of carefully worked stone points.

By about 5000–6000 BCE both the prairie and woodland parts of the state were home to early Native Americans. In the Prairie Lake region of western Minnesota, scattered groups of people hunted buffalo, domesticated dogs, and processed wild grains with hand mills. The people probably established a number of seasonal camps in different areas that allowed them to take advantage of various resources. Several sites have been uncovered on islands in shallow prairie lakes that would have allowed summer fishing and provided a measure of protection against any enemies. In eastern Minnesota, rivers and lakes provided excellent highways for early Woodland peoples. By 3000 BCE they had become established as far north as the Ontario border.

In both the Woodland and Prairie Archaic phases, men and women made and used a variety of sophisticated stone and bone tools that allowed them effectively to exploit their environment, be it lakes, open prairie, forests, or wooded river bottoms. In addition to woven baskets, they made sand- and shell-tempered pottery decorated with embossed marks in complex horizontal, vertical, and oblique motifs. Beginning about 5000 BCE, natives living near Lake Superior developed copper tools and jewelry. Using nuggets of copper found on the surface, they shaped the metal with a simple process of pounding and annealing the copper nuggets into useful and beautiful objects.

WOODLAND CULTURE

By about 2,500 years ago, at the beginning of what archeologists call the Woodland Period, the practice of burying the dead in mounds spread throughout the region as populations steadily increased, though this was most common in the eastern sections of the state. The first mounds date from around 690 BCE Although the practice had long since ceased by historic times, such burial mounds were once common across the upper Midwest, with 11,000 in Minnesota alone. While most have since been lost to development and agriculture, as well as amateur souvenir seekers and would-be archeologists, a few preserved examples remain, such as Grand Mound State Historic Site along the Rainy River in northern Minnesota. Grand Mound is 25 feet high, 100 by 140 feet at the base, containing 5,000 tons of earth. It developed gradually over hundreds of years, as local people brought the bones of their dead to be buried there (perhaps after first exposing the bodies for a time on raised platforms). Perhaps as many 5,500 people were interred there.

Minnesota seems to have been on the western periphery of the great mound-building cultures of the Ohio River region, where large and well-settled peoples developed mounds in the shape of animals and birds. A few of these types of mounds once existed in the state along the Wisconsin border, but all have been lost and only a few long, linear mounds have been preserved. If mound-building can be taken as a sign of population density, the Mississippi valley was probably the most settled part of the state. At Prairie Island, near Red Wing, native peoples occupied scores of sites on both sides of the valley, both on bluffs and in the river bottoms. (Prairie Island is a relatively rare example of a site that has remained almost continuously inhabited for many centuries.)

Evidence of the region's early inhabitants can also be seen in petroglyphs carved on rock outcroppings throughout the state. Perhaps the best known and largest site is the Jeffers Petroglyphs, a state historic site in southwestern Minnesota. Carvings of human figures shown bearing atlatls (spear throwers) date the first petroglyphs at 2,500 to 5,000 years. Native peoples continued to chisel religious symbols into the red Sioux Quartzite, called caitlinite, into historic times, although the meanings of the symbols probably did not remain fixed.

Establishing continuity between the ancient carvings and more recent practices is fraught with difficulty. The carvings were representations of powerful spiritual concepts, such as the visions of shamans experiencing states of altered consciousness. Many were carved based on such visions and were not meant as public art. Certain symbols and motifs appear in many Upper Midwest rock carvings, including at Jeffers. Some were depictions of shamanistic rituals and altered states of reality: figures with upraised arms, "medicine bags," figures with elongated bodies or extra fingers and toes, and figures that are half human and half animal. Others were pictures of spirit beings or mythic figures: the Horned Serpent, Thunderbirds, or the Ojibwe mythic figure Nanaboujou.

Must-See Sites: Forest History Center, Grand Rapids

Visit a recreated turn-of-the-century logging camp and find the camp blacksmith, saw filer, clerk, cook, and lumberjacks. Visitors can board the moored "wanigan," a floating cook shack used when the logs and men headed downstream to the mills. There is also a 1930s Minnesota Forest Service patrolman's cabin and lookout tower where visitors can learn about the ranger's important work protecting woodland resources. Self-guided forest trails and museum exhibits complete the story of life in the northern forests of Minnesota from ancient times to today.

Contact: (218) 327-4482; E-mail: foresthistory@mnhs.org; Web: www.mnhs.org

Location: Near U.S. Hwys 169 & 2. 2609 County Road 76, Grand Rapids

Another key Native American site is the Pipestone National Monument in southwestern Minnesota. Although the site may have been occupied as early as the Woodland Period, based on some archeological finds and petroglyphs, Pipestone's most important days began around 1600 CE, when native people quarried the red Sioux Quartzite to make ceremonial pipes. The red rock is relatively soft and easy to carve. Pink when taken from the ground, it gradually becomes dark red on exposure to air. Pipestone had enormous religious significance to many native groups and was open to all tribes—a place of peace where long-standing rivals could mine the sacred stone side by side. Pipes made of this stone were important trade items and have been found as far away as the southeastern United States.

MISSISSIPPI PERIOD

By about 900 CE, agricultural production was introduced in the form of maize cultivation, which set off a far-reaching set of cultural and technological changes as shown by archeological evidence (called the Mississippi Period). New peoples moved in, not always peacefully, and the existing Woodland cultures were transformed. Trade grew as products from other regions of North America, such as tobacco, were brought in and local items (copper or pipestone, for example) were bartered out.

As would become clear during the fur trade era, the importance of trade for the native people was less for commerce in its own right than for its role in a culture where politics was often linked to chains of reciprocal gift giving. Leaders or chiefs (a term adapted from the French who were the first Europeans to describe and participate in this system) gained support through gift giving and thus relied on trade to supply rare or unusual items. As a result of this, political power was often highly diffuse and chiefs were left to rely on persuasion rather than coercion. Their power was limited and their ability to command loyalty often lasted only for as long as they could supply presents. Some native cultures in North America did develop more hierarchical systems of leadership, similar to the cultures of Central and South America, but, as far as scholars can tell, not the peoples of the Great Lakes and Great Plains regions.

It is a perilous exercise to link the many prehistoric cultures as identified by archeologists to the historic peoples known to be living in the region at the time of European contact; in recent decades this same exercise has become more than a little political. Native inhabitants of the region were often highly mobile and their cultures subject to the same processes of change as anyone else. Prior to the arrival of the first Frenchmen in the 1600s, European ideas and technology had entered the region and had been adapted and altered by the native peoples to suit their own needs. Nevertheless, by the 1600s, the region had been inhabited for several thousand years and its people had developed their own cultural, religious, political, and economic systems that were well adapted to the world in which they lived.

THE OJIBWE

At the time of European contact, the Minnesota region was home to two large tribal groups, both of which were part of a larger ethnolinguistic family. Northern Minnesota was home to the Ojibwe or Ojibway (formerly called the Chippewa and known in their own language as Anishinabe or "first people"). Ojibwe are Algonquin speakers, part of a large and diverse family of native tribes that at one time could be found from Virginia to New England, and from eastern Canada throughout the Great Lakes and west to the foothills of the Rocky Mountains. Southern Minnesota was home to the Dakota, one dialectical part of the Sioux nation, a large and closely related group that consists of several tribes speaking three dialects: Dakota, Lakota, and Nakota. They lived from the western fringes of the Great Lakes to the Rocky Mountains and from the prairies of southern Canada south to Nebraska. In addition, Minnesota has occasionally been a partial home to some small tribes, such as the Ho-Chunk (or Winnebago).

According to one oral tradition, the ancestors of the Ojibwe migrated into northern Minnesota from the east, possibly from the Atlantic coast, across Ontario to Lake Huron, then to Sault Ste. Marie, and finally to western Lake Superior and northern Minnesota. Although no chronology can be attached to this tradition, it is likely that such a migration began before 1492. The tribe was divided into some twenty-one clans, of which six were major clans: Catfish, Crane, Loon, Bear, Wolf, and Marten, which in the

middle of the nineteenth century made up about 80 percent of Ojibwe. As in many cultures where clan structures exist, the clans implied a common ancestry though not necessarily close blood relations. The Ojibwe retained a unique wrinkle in this system in that it was always considered taboo to marry within the same clan.

On arriving in the region, the tribe established a major center at La Pointe (today Madeline Island, the largest of Wisconsin's Apostle Islands), possibly by the late 1400s. From there, they dispersed throughout the Lake Superior region. The Ojibwe were divided by geography into groups, each developing distinct economies. Those in the northern-most forests relied more heavily on hunting and later trapping. Ojibwe on the southern and western shores of Superior relied more on fishing, while those in the interior of Minnesota and northern Wisconsin depended the most on wild rice.

Wild rice was the most important and culturally significant food for Minnesota's early native peoples. A grain that grows wild around the shores of many northern lakes, wild rice occurs in such abundance that it does not need to be sown like other cereals, though the Native Americans who harvested it used methods that ensured a certain amount always returned to seed for the following year. Although some wild rice is today grown commercially in California, in Minnesota and Wisconsin it remains a naturally sown plant that by law is harvested and sold only by Native Americans. Wild rice is considered a sacred plant by most Native Americans of the Upper Midwest, one given to them as a special gift from Great Spirit. It was a grain said to have been given Native Americans "just as other foods were given to whites." Since the Ojibwe moved into northern Minnesota it has played an important role in major ceremonies and life passages of the people and has sometimes been buried with the dead.

In addition to hunting, fishing, and ricing, Ojibwe gathered a vast array of plants, particularly berries, herbs, acorns, and tubers. They also grew gardens of corn, pumpkins, and squash. Later, they also made maple sugar. (When exactly Native Americans began to make maple sugar is unknown but it was probably after European

Ojibwe Elder, circa 1915

contact.) Ojibwe lived in permanent villages, although temporary encampments while traveling or hunting were also known. Wigwams were the main village dwelling, consisting of a wooden frame, shaped like an elongated dome, covered with rushes or birch bark. Ojibwe were masters at using tree bark in large quantities, not only to make coverings for their wigwams, but also to create a variety of useful items, including the birch bark canoe, which was easy to paddle and light enough for a man to carry when portaging between lakes or around rapids.

Ojibwe society was matrilocal and like many hunting, gathering, and pre-industrial agricultural societies, there were strict gender divisions in terms of labor and responsibilities. Although such an arrangement is alien to modern Americans, it provided these societies with a certain order and coherence in harsh and difficult conditions. It also tended to divide rights and duties up in ways that to modern eyes often seem surprisingly equitable. In Ojibwe society—as in many such cultures—there was little margin for those who were lazy, and no one could expect to survive without cooperating. So, for example, hunting was largely reserved for men, while the gathering and processing of wild rice was done almost entirely by women up until the last few decades.

As the Ojibwe moved into Minnesota and Wisconsin and dispersed outward from their main center at La Pointe, they found other resident tribes, in particular the Dakota and Fox, which often resulted in intense conflicts. Politicized scholarship has in the past portrayed Native Americans as either completely warlike or, until the coming of the "white man," completely peaceful. In reality, they were no more or less warlike than most cultures. Warfare often consisted of lightning raids on enemy villages to take prisoners and trophies such as scalps. However, it was not unknown for whole villages to be destroyed, and in one Ojibwe legend, for warriors to destroy almost an entire tribe who—the legend said—were particularly wicked. In some cases, the Ojibwe tortured and killed their captives, but more often, and less remembered, they absorbed them into the tribe. In particular, they simply adopted and enculturated young captive children.

The Ojibwe were more successful warriors than most, perhaps due in part to the fact that they were an especially large tribe. They drove the Fox out of northwest Wisconsin and the St. Croix valley and by the middle of the eighteenth century had pushed the Dakota out of much of northern Minnesota. The latter achievement is particularly noteworthy, since the Ojibwe can claim to be the only Native American tribe to have truly defeated a part of the formidable Sioux nation. Although courage and daring had much to do with this victory, the Ojibwe's acquisition of firearms from French traders was just as important—they were among the first tribes to possess firearms.

A detailed, blow-by-blow history of the Ojibwe–Dakota conflict is impossible to reconstruct, but the general outlines are clear. There were at least two major battles already in the seventeenth century, and the eighteenth century witnessed some of the fiercest struggles. Not all contact between the two groups was conflict. In the early stages, the Ojibwe provided a conduit for European trade goods to the Dakota. However, as the French presence grew, the Dakota came to resent the favoritism shown to their rivals, the Ojibwe, Cree, and Assiniboine. Dakota attacks on French traders only further cemented French–Ojibwe friendship. In return, the Dakota would eventually find allies among British traders.

In the centuries to come, neither the Ojibwe nor the Dakota would forget their respective European allies. They retained a nostalgic attachment to them that contrasted sharply with hatred of the seemingly rapacious Americans. One French explorer, Joseph Nicollet, recalled a conversation with a group of Ojibwe in the 1830s who told him:

> Our fathers always said they would love to see the French from France again, they who discovered this land and who were the first to be good to us.... There ensued a long conversation about their missing French, on the excitement caused by my presence among them, on the inner fire kindled by the French who provided a great well-being.... They presented me with a calumet of peace and friendship for the king of France, urging me to talk with him for a long time on their behalf.

An Englishman, Frederick Marryat, traveling in the region at about the same time, had a similar encounter with a group of Dakota who told him: "You are an Englishman and a warrior in your own country. You cross the great waters as fast as we can our prairies. We recollect the English, and we like them; they used us well. The rifles and blankets which they gave us, according to promise, were of good quality: not like the American goods.... The English keep their word, and they live in our memory." Even into the late nineteenth and early twentieth centuries, it was not uncommon to encounter Native Americans in the Upper Midwest who proudly bore uniforms, medals, or flags handed down from the time of European encounter.

Although the British and French each played a role in the Dakota–Ojibwe conflict, and despite sporadic efforts to broker peace deals that would benefit trade, representatives of both countries were secondary players. Not until the Americans established a large presence in Minnesota in the 1830s and 1840s would an outside power have the means to significantly affect the conflict. The war was fought among Native Americans, sparked by their concerns and desires, and not by outside agents.

In 1736 the Ojibwe opened a new phase of the war by launching a concerted attack on the Dakota in north-central and central Minnesota. At stake were the forest lands east of the Mississippi, lands rich in resources and coveted by both groups. The offensive forced the large, but more scattered, Dakota southward. By 1750, the Mdewakanton Dakota were forced out of the area around Mille Lacs.

In 1768, the Dakota gathered a force of some 500 warriors near the site of present-day Minneapolis for a counteroffensive. A large Dakota attacking force slipped into the heart of the Ojibwe area, bypassing outlying settlements. Following the path of the Crow Wing River and portaging their canoes to Cass Lake and Leech Lake, they hoped to descend back down the Mississippi, using the element of surprise, raiding as they went. This daring maneuver at first met with success and the Dakota fell on and slew a few isolated hunters and groups of people out gathering food. They also captured a group of about thirty, mostly young, women.

Native American girl with baby in a cradleboard, 1930

Papoose,
Park Rapids, Min

At the Sandy Lake Ojibwe village, however, their luck began to change. The village was alerted to the attack and although many of its best fighters were away on a raid against the Dakota, the remaining inhabitants put up fierce resistance and drove the attackers off. The Dakota then fell back down the Mississippi, bearing their captives.

In the meantime, however, an Ojibwe raiding party had come across signs of the earlier Dakota passage and though badly outnumbered set up an ambush at the confluence of the Crow Wing and Mississippi Rivers, just south of present-day Brainerd. They dug rifle pits on the bluffs overlooking the rivers and attacked the unsuspecting Dakota while they sailed past in their canoes, throwing the Dakota into confusion. At this moment, the captive Ojibwe women deliberately capsized the canoes they were in and swam to shore, leaving their erstwhile captors floundering in the water under a hail of musketry and arrows. The Dakota regrouped and counterattacked, but the Ojibwe were well entrenched, held the high ground, and repulsed every effort, although the Dakota managed to retain a few captives. Defeated, the Dakota fell back to the south. Although raids and battles would continue for many decades, after the loss at the Battle of Crow Wing, the Dakota largely abandoned the area east of the Mississippi and took up residence along the Minnesota River.

The Dakota

The Dakota people the Ojibwe battled were the oldest-known native inhabitants of Minnesota and a people possessing a rich and ancient culture. A cultural continuity with the Dakota presence in the state is traceable from at least the end of the Woodland period (about 1,200 to 1,300 years ago). Minnesota's name derives from the Dakota dialect, variously translated as "Land of Sky-Colored Waters" or "Land of Waters that Reflect the Sky."

The Dakota are a tribal and linguistic segment of the Sioux nation. Although the term Sioux is a bit of a misnomer, having been applied by the Ojibwe, it has come to encompass a large native group consisting of eight major tribes: Mdewakanton ("Spirit Lake People"), Wahpeton ("Dwellers among the Leaves"), Wahpekute ("Shooters among the Leaves"), Sisseton ("People of the Boggy

Ground"), Yankton ("People at the End Village"), Yankonai ("Little People at the End"), Assiniboin ("Stony"), and Teton ("Dwellers on the Plains"). The Tetons are further divided into seven tribes: Brule/Sicangu (or "Burnt Thighs"), Oglala ("They Scatter Their Own"), Oohenonpa ("Two Kettles"), Minneconjou ("Planters Beside the Water"), Sans Arc/Itazipco ("Those without Bows"), Hunkpapa ("Campers at the Horn"), and Sihasapa ("Blackfoot"). The Sioux speak three related and mutually intelligible dialects: Dakota (spoken by the Mdewakanton, Wahpeton, Wahpekute, and Sisseton), Lakota (spoken by the seven tribes of the Teton), and Nakota (spoken by the Sisseton, Yankton, and Yankonai). The three dialects are part of an even larger family of Native American languages called Siouian. The Sioux are perhaps the best-known Native Americans, in part due to the dubious attention of Hollywood and to the fact that they put up the longest and most successful resistance to American expansion.

Although the term "Sioux" conjures up images of the Great Plains for many, Minnesota's Dakota people initially lived in a mixed landscape of forest, lake, and prairie. Although perhaps never as sedentary as the Ojibwe, the Dakota were not simply nomads who followed buffalo herds. Their diverse landscape provided a variety of resources at different times of the year. During their tenure in northern Minnesota, for example, they are known to have harvested wild rice and had relied on the grain for at least as long as other tribes. Even after they were driven from the major ricing lakes east of the Mississippi, they continued the practice in southern Minnesota in far more restricted circumstances.

The Dakota had a kind of semi-nomadic lifestyle in which they lived in a variety of temporary villages throughout the year, sometimes but not always in the same locations each season. There was a yearly cycle of activities. In the fall, they harvested gardens for their corn and vegetables and then scattered into small winter camps consisting of three or four families, and spent the winter sheltering in wooded areas, such as along the Minnesota River. They came together again in the spring. Scattering in winter made sense since it was less likely to tax resources in any one area. From October to January, the men hunted

deer. The Dakota also relied on many small animals, such as the muskrat, which was hunted in the late winter or early spring. As in many tribes, they also consumed dog meat. One American observer, missionary Samuel Pond, wrote: "It is well known that dog-flesh was considered a delicacy by them, but it was seldom eaten except on great occasions. The writer had determined never to taste canine flesh, but his Native American friends contrived to have him eat it

Corn, Northfield

unwittingly, and he was compelled to admit it was very good." In the spring, tribes tapped maple trees when fur trapping was at its height. By the late spring, when the first wild strawberries appeared, they planted corn. In the summer, bands scattered again to search for food in diverse areas. This was the time of the buffalo hunt for men. For

Must-See Sites: Pipestone National Monument, Pipestone

For centuries one of the most important cultural sites for the Northern Plains Indians, Pipestone was declared a national monument in 1937. Here, native peoples quarried the soft red stone known as caitlinite, which was used to make sacred pipes. This stone has been found among Native Americans as far away as South Carolina. Inseparable from the traditions that structured daily routine and honored the spirit world, pipes figured prominently in the ways of the village and in dealings between tribes. The story parallels that of a culture in transition: The evolution of the pipes influenced, and was influenced by, their makers' association with white explorers, traders, soldiers, and settlers. Plains Indian culture has undergone radical change since the era of the free-ranging buffalo herds, yet pipe carving is by no means a lost art. Carvings today are considered significant both as art and for ceremonial uses, and the pipestone here is quarried by anyone of Native American ancestry. The National Monument tells the story of an age-old tradition that continues in the modern world, ever-changing yet firmly rooted in the past.

Contact: (507) 825-5464; Web: www.nps.gov/pipe/

Location: Just outside of Pipestone.

women, as historians Alan and Nancy Woolworth wrote, "They diligently sought out everything edible whether it grew on bushes or trees, on the ground, or in mud at the bottom of lakes. While some were digging all day on the prairies for a peck of wild turnips, others were in the water up to their arms, exploring the bottom of lakes in search of roots."

Although semi-permanent wigwams were used in the summer, most Dakota lived in teepees, a conical wood frame covered with skins that was well-suited to their lifestyle. Easy to move and set up, it was a happy medium between the need for comfort and shelter and the need for mobility. Belongings could easily be packed up and placed on travois, which were often pulled by dogs.

Even observers who were not always sympathetic to the Native Americans, such as the missionary Pond, were impressed with the economy of the Dakota: "the experience of a few months residence with the Dakotas, in their own teepees, opened my eyes to many things I should not otherwise have seen. Among other things that were new to me, I learned that they kept as good a lookout for the future as their mode of life would admit. Nothing was wasted…. And while we were declaiming against the improvident habits of the Indians, they were astonished at our wastefulness."

The notion of Native Americans as conservators of nature is a modern notion whose terms of reference would have been alien to a people who did not see a separation between "humanity" and "nature" and did not view the world as a finite thing to be "conserved," even though hunger and privation were common. The impulse to use a resource as fully as possible arose out of necessity. If a hunter took a deer, he did not know when he would find the next one. Prior to the arrival of the horse, however, natives of the plains used fire or simple enclosure to funnel herds of buffalo into killing zones, often running them off cliffs, hardly a practice that would find favor with the modern environmentalist.

The great economic and cultural revolution for the peoples of the plains came in the mid eighteenth century with the introduction of the horse. Horses that escaped from the Spanish in Mexico bred wild and spread north or were captured and traded by native peoples. The horse allowed the Sioux and other plains peoples far more efficient and reliable buffalo hunting, which in turn allowed more time and resources for cultural pursuits. It also made them some of the greatest horsemen the world has ever seen. A Sioux warrior riding at full gallop could loose an arrow and have a second arrow in the air by the time the first one struck its mark. In Minnesota, the horse had the greatest impact on the Lakota and Nakota peoples who lived in the far western part of the state prior to the wars with the Ojibwe. After the Dakota were driven out of the north country, the Lakota and Nakota also moved further west into what is now North and South Dakota. As a people who lived on the forest-prairie margin and not as reliant on buffalo, the Dakota were not as dramatically affected by the arrival of the horse, although the animal grew more important as they moved farther west.

Must-See Sites: Mille Lacs Indian Museum, Onamia

The Mille Lacs Indian Museum opened May 18, 1996. It offers exhibits dedicated to the story of the Mille Lacs Band of Ojibwe, from their first journey to Minnesota to the present. Videos, computer interactive displays, listening stations, and objects reveal information about the band's life today, from how dance traditions are carried on to members' interests in music to sovereignty issues. The museum's spacious crafts room serves as a demonstration area for traditional cooking, birch-bark basketry, and beadwork. The building's arching window wall reflects the shoreline of Lake Mille Lacs. Fashioned in cedar, the exterior is highlighted with a copper dome and an inset tile band designed by Mille Lacs elder Batiste Sam. Adjacent to the museum, a restored trading post retains its 1930s appearance. Here visitors find American Indian gifts from Mille Lacs artisans.

Contact: (320) 532-3632; E-mail: millelacs@mnhs.org; Web: www.mnhs.org

Location: 12 miles north of Onamia on the southwest shore of Lake Mille Lacs (U.S. Hwy 169).

In the wake of the wars with the Ojibwe and at the time of European contact, the Dakota occupied southeastern, south-central, and southwestern Minnesota. They consisted of two main groups. The Mdewakanton were the easternmost of the Dakota, with settlements as far east as present-day St. Paul, but they could also be found in the Minnesota River Valley. The Santee band of the Sisseton lived in southwestern Minnesota, along the present-day Minnesota–South Dakota border. The area was also occasionally home to some Yankton Nakota, and some Wahpeton and Wahpetkute lived in the Red River Valley.

In addition to the Ojibwe and Dakota, a few other Native American groups were found in Minnesota in the nineteenth century as a result of dislocations caused by conflicts further east. After being pushed out of the Great Lakes region, bands of Sac and Fox were sometimes found in southern Minnesota, whether raiding or hunting, though their main home at that time was Iowa. The Ho-Chunk people (formerly called the Winnebago) were moved into central Minnesota and later south-central Minnesota, near the present-day city of Mankato, as part of a series of U.S. government-forced relocations. Prior to that, they had lived in Wisconsin, including the Mississippi River Valley.

Much has been written about Native Americans and their subsequent treatment, some of it worthwhile, some of it not. In more recent times, the skein has become more confused, which is reflected in the various names of tribes and of the people themselves: Indians, Native Americans, First Nations, Indigenous Peoples, and so on. There has always been a tendency to either romanticize or demonize Native Americans. In more recent times, the romantic view has won out, but whether this represents an improvement in historical writing is questionable. Minnesota's first inhabitants were neither "savages" nor noble, spiritual caretakers of the environment, but peoples with complex and interesting histories who were intrinsically no better and no worse than anyone else. Understanding this makes the story of the tragedies that befell them all the more poignant.

3

PAYS D'EN HAUT: EXPLORATION, FUR TRADE, AND EMPIRE, 1650–1849

The first Europeans to set foot in what is now Minnesota were Frenchmen who probably arrived in the 1650s. They were explorers, missionaries, and traders traveling through a land they referred to as the Upper Country—Pays d'en Haut.

Their arrival in Minnesota was part of a process of expanding European power, tied to the growing strength of monarchies and the influence of merchants and bankers who financed the plans of the continent's sovereigns. The first major European encounter with the Western Hemisphere occurred in 1492, with the first voyage of Christopher Columbus. Prior to that, a settlement of Scandinavian Vikings had been briefly and unsuccessfully established on the northern tip of Newfoundland. By the 1450s Basque fisherman may have been aware of the New World by fishing in the Grand Banks. Portuguese explorers may have discovered Brazil a generation before Columbus, but kept it secret when they realized it was not India and that its revelation to European rivals would have tipped everyone off to their eventually successful plan to reach India via a voyage around Africa. According to a few Minnesotans, mostly of Scandinavian descent, the state was discovered by a party of Vikings in the 1380s who left behind the so-called Kensington Runestone "discovered" near Alexandria in the 1890s. Few take such claims seriously.

Although the British, Spanish, Dutch, French, and Swedes all staked claims to part of North America in the sixteenth and seventeenth centuries, few managed to penetrate the heart of the continent prior to the 1650s. A few early Spanish expeditions reached as far north as Kansas, but this success was fleeting and the Spanish preferred to concentrate on Central America, the southwest, and the west coast, though Spain did technically rule part of Minnesota in the late eighteenth century. Yet it was the French who were first able to traverse the center of North America through their control of two great waterways, the Mississippi and the Great Lakes. This not only gave the French a fifty-year head start on their rivals, it also made them the first Europeans to reach the western Great Lakes and Minnesota.

THE FRENCH LEGACY

Evidence of the French legacy can be seen on any Minnesota map in dozens of harmonious-sounding place names: St. Croix ("Holy Cross"), St. Louis, Duluth, Superior, Grand Portage, Grand Marais, Mille Lacs, Pomme de Terre ("Potato"), Cloquet, Faribault, Le Sueur, Belle Plaine (Beautiful Field), Traverse des Sioux (Sioux Crossing), Lac qui Parle (Treaty Lake). Many other places have had their French names translated into English, but we still know them by the appellations these often unknown Frenchmen gave them.

The French journey to Minnesota began in 1535 with the discovery of the St. Lawrence River by explorer Jacques Cartier. Until the end of the sixteenth century, however, Spain dominated New World colonization and little profit could be imagined from cold northern lands. Nevertheless, the lure of riches, the vision of a sea passage through the continent, and the desire for national glory drew the major European seafaring powers to North America. By 1600, the first permanent French post was founded in Canada. Quebec was founded in 1608 and Trois Rivères in 1634. Following the path of the inland water, French progress was rapid and Crown officials claimed a vast inland territory under the colors of the Fleur de Lis. By 1639 the French had reached Ste. Sault Marie and Lake Superior. By 1659, the first recorded French exploration penetrated the western shores of the great lake.

Pierre Esprit Radisson and his brother-in-law Médard Chouart Sieur de Groseilliers traveled across Lake Superior, following the north coast of what is now Michigan's Upper Peninsula until they reached Madeline Island in the Apostle Chain. Groseilliers had previously journeyed to Lake Superior and Lake Michigan in 1654, but this trip was probably the first western journey of the younger Radisson. From there, they journeyed somewhere to the west, reaching the territory of the Dakota people— the "people of the beef" as Radisson called them—before returning to Quebec in the summer of 1660. The pair may not have been the first Frenchmen to reach the area, but their expedition was the first to leave a somewhat reliable written record. Still, the newness and beauty of the land they traveled through amazed them. Radisson later wrote:

> I can assure you I liked no country as I have the one where in we wintered, for whatever a man can desire was to be had in great plenty, viz., stags, fishes in abundance, and all sorts of meat, corn enough.... We embarked ourselves on the delightsomest lake of the world. I took notice of their cottages and of the journeys of our navigation because the country was so pleasant, so beautiful, and so fruitful that it grieved me to see that the world could not discover such enticing countries to live in. This I say because the Europeans fight for a rock in the sea against one another, or for a sterile land and horrid country that the people sent here or there by the changement of the air engenders sickness and dies thereof. Contrawise, these kingdoms are so delicious and under so temperate a climate, plentiful in all things, the earth bringing forth its fruit twice a year, the people living long and lusty and wise in their way.

Radisson was more than a little prone to exaggeration for he and Groseilliers also witnessed winter starvation among the Native Americans they lived with. Throughout they were treated with wary respect by the tribes they visited and were sometimes called on to hear disputes between them. Radisson crowed: "We were Caesars, being nobody to contradict us."

In 1673 Louis Jolliet and Fr. Jacques Marquette landed at Green Bay and then pushed west across Wisconsin, reaching the Mississippi River. Five years later, an expedition led by Daniel Greysolon Sieur Du Luth, landed at the southwest end of Lake Superior, at the site of a modern city that bears his name (Duluth). He met the Dakota people and journeyed south with his men to Lake Mille Lacs, claiming the entire country for the French King Louis XIV. He and his men also heard rumors of a large body of salt water to the west—or at least reported these rumors. Inspired by a vision of a route to the Pacific and by the potential of the fur trade in the western Great Lakes, the French would send a series of expeditions to the region.

Fr. Louis Hennepin, a Francophone Belgian Franciscan priest of the Recollect Order, traveled as a missionary with the French explorer Robert Cavalier Sieur de la Salle in 1680. He and two companions separated from La Salle's expedition and were soon captured or met up with a group of Dakota (accounts differ). Brought north along the Mississippi, Fr. Hennepin was the first European to reach the site of what would become the state's largest city, Minneapolis. There, Hennepin wrote:

> Navigation is interrupted ten or twelve leagues upstream by a waterfall. I named it the Falls of St. Anthony of Padua in gratitude for favors God did me through the intercession of that great saint, whom we chose as patron and protector of all our enterprises. The waterfall is forty or fifty feet high and has a small rocky island, shaped like the pyramid, in the center.

Later, Hennepin and his guides reached Mille Lacs:

> The lake spreads over vast swamps where wild rice grows.... This kind of grain grows in swampy land without being sown. It resembles oats but tastes better and has longer stems and stalks. The Native Americans gather it in season, the women binding many stalks together with basswood bark to prevent its being entirely eaten by flocks of duck and teal found in the region. The Native Americans lay in a store of it for part of the year, to eat when the hunting season is over.

Although Hennepin overestimated the height of St. Anthony Falls, when he returned to Europe his account was the first published report to provide descriptions of the region to the reading public.

A permanent French outpost was established in the 1680s on the Wisconsin side of Lake Pepin on the Mississippi River, which provided a base for trading and exploration into southern and central Minnesota and Iowa. In 1700, Pierre Charles Le Sueur traveled north from the mouth of the Mississippi to the Minnesota River and then to the Blue Earth River near present day Mankato. There, Le Sueur set up a small outpost, Fort L'Huiller, and proceeded to search for copper deposits. Since his orders did not permit him to gather furs, it is likely that the copper deposits were simply a convenient excuse to circumvent this prohibition. Le Sueur's copper never made it to France, but some 4,000 furs did. His fort was abandoned the following year, though his name lives on in the name of a river and a county. Following the war of Spanish Succession, which caused the French to withdraw from the western lakes until after 1713, a new expedition to southern Minnesota in 1721 established a short-lived outpost on the Minnesota shores of Lake Pepin. Some French occupation continued at this site throughout the 1720s before it was abandoned.

Although French traders were in northern Minnesota from a very early date, the first permanent French outposts there were founded in the 1730s. Of these, Grand Portage, founded in 1732, was the most important since it stood at the Lake Superior end of a nine-mile portage that connected the Great Lakes to a chain of waterways leading to the northern Great Plains, the Rocky Mountains, and north to Lake Winnipeg and Hudson's Bay. That same year La Vérendrye and his sons founded Fort St. Charles on Lake of Woods, in the Northwest Angle near the modern U.S.–Canadian border.

UNDER THE UNION JACK

In 1759 French power in North America suffered a mortal blow with the fall of Quebec to the British, and Canada was lost for good in 1763. French Canada had survived for 150 years despite a small population base and in the face of the British navy, which severely restricted trade. It ultimately proved untenable in spite of the courage and tenacity of many of its adherents. Nevertheless, when the Fleur de Lis was lowered for the last time over French forts on the Great Lakes it did not spell the end of the French impact on Minnesota and the surrounding region. Ironically, more Frenchmen and Métis probably came to Minnesota under British rule than had under French control.

Early explorers and missionaries were followed by the fur traders. Their first outposts were often little more than a few huts with a warehouse and perhaps a smithy to repair metal goods for traders and local Native Americans, all surrounded by a wooden stockade. As the fur trade in Minnesota reached its height under the British, some of its outposts became small bustling towns, at least during part of the year.

European passion for beaver pelts and a desire for empire may have stimulated the fur trade, but it was always a joint Native American–European venture. Both sides derived advantage from it, and contrary to popular belief it was not merely a case of clever Europeans duping simple Native Americans. Despite Radisson's statement, the European fur traders were hardly "Caesars"; the trade would not have existed without the agreement and participation of the native peoples of the Pays d'en Haut.

Both Native Americans and Europeans brought different expectations and outlooks to the relationship, but in time, as historian Richard White describes, the two worlds met and merged, intertwining ideas and objects to the extent that it is often impossible if not futile to identify that which is "purely" European or "purely" indigenous.

For the Native Americans, the trade brought European goods that made life marginally easier, but these goods were used and understood within a native context. As in centuries past, commerce was seen as a system of reciprocal gift giving. Europeans clearly possessed political, technological, and perhaps even spiritual power, but to the Native Americans the powerful could never directly command and their authority could only be maintained through gift giving. The powerful were required to be generous, and those who were not generous could not be truly powerful. Those who did not give gifts became the objects of resentment, ingrates and misers to whom little respect could be shown.

Native peoples saw in Europeans an unknown element that they gradually incorporated into their own world. Gift giving was part of this process. The language that Native Americans used to describe French or English authority, that is, of European "fathers" and native "children" also caught the sense of this obligation: Good fathers were supposed to provide for their children and treat them with kindness. In addition, "fathers" were called on to resolve disputes between rival tribes. This not only further drew the Europeans into the Native American world, but resulted in political advantage and further opportunities for gift giving. Each treaty had to be sealed with gifts and revenge killings were averted by "covering" those killed in war with more gifts. Finally, Native Americans drew Europeans directly into their kinship networks through the marriages of native women to European traders.

For the Europeans, the politics of gift giving often had the opposite meaning. The weak gave gifts to placate the powerful or win favors. Both the French and British (and later the Americans) were indeed powerful, but in the eighteenth century and even into the nineteenth century, sending large bodies of troops into the Upper Country was costly, logistically difficult, and usually futile. At best, the French and British could maintain a few fortified outposts in the region, more often to guard against each other than against "hostile" Native Americans. In order to conduct the fur trade it was necessary to gain the cooperation of the native peoples and this could only be done through a regular supply of gifts. By giving gifts, the Europeans created a chain of obligation. Chiefs who received gifts could in turn distribute them to followers, relatives, and allies, thus enhancing their own prestige.

This gift giving was necessary because, as archeological evidence has shown, native peoples of the Great Lakes were by no means dependent on European trade goods. Although the goods made life easier and more comfortable, the Native Americans could just as easily do without. Old technologies and skills were maintained alongside new innovations and products. Since trapping beaver in exchange for trade goods was not something the Native Americans needed to do for survival, the chain of gift giving was a necessary lubricant and inducement to participate in the trade. Some trade goods had a more dangerous effect. Liquor was the most obvious example. In the beginning, the French tried to stop its sale to the Native Americans, but the British had no such qualms and used alcohol as a wedge to enter French markets. Soon competition and demand from the tribes forced the French to loosen their restrictions. The debate continues over the cultural and physiological impact of the liquor trade on the Native Americans, but it is clear that the net effect was very bad indeed.

The process of European–Native American relations did not always proceed smoothly and was marked by cultural misunderstanding and political mistakes on both sides. The French, however, were the first Europeans to attempt to understand the native cultures of the Pays d'en Haut and perhaps, of the Europeans, understood it best. A later English observer wrote that the French voyageurs "adopted the very Principles and Ideas of the Native Americans and differ from them only a Little in color." Another found that the French "almost became one People with them." Although perhaps exaggerated a bit, fur trade and exploration were possible only through a mutual process of cultural and political mediation. As historian Richard White put it, it was a "mutually comprehensible, jointly invented world rather than a traditional set of procedures" imposed by one side or the other. In time, both came to view it a natural state of affairs.

THE FUR TRADE

Aside from the Native Americans themselves, the key actors were those who conducted the fur trade, especially the voyageurs who yet stand as the most colorful and legendary figures in the history of the north country. The term *voyageur* simply means traveler and came to denote one of the licensed canoemen, traders, and porters who made the fur trade possible. The voyageurs often knew themselves simply as *engagés* (or "employees") of a fur trading company. They were further divided into classes: The *mangeurs du lard* ("pork eaters") were less experienced while the *hivernants* ("hibernators") were old hands who could winter over in the north woods. *Voyageurs* were licensed, but unlicensed traders or *coureurs de bois* ("woods runners") were not unknown either.

If the Native Americans were not always eager to hunt the furs that Europe demanded, then they were even less willing to brave a long journey across the Great Lakes past potentially hostile rivals in all sorts of weather to deliver furs to trading centers or outposts such as Detroit, Montreal, or Oswego. Recurring wars between Iroquois and Algonquin tribes often stopped such journeys altogether. If the Native

Two fur traders, 1880

Americans would not come to Montreal and Detroit, it was decided, why not bring the trade to the Native Americans themselves, in their own villages? Thus, the need for tough, resourceful canoemen was born.

The French desire to export Great Lakes fur (either through Canada or south down the Mississippi to New Orleans) was challenged by British traders from the east coast colonies and from the north by the Hudson's Bay Company, a British corporation founded at the suggestion of Frenchmen and staffed largely by Scots. Later, the British would displace the French from Canada and then the Americans would displace the British from the east coast. Each of these rivals, however, relied on the same pool of men drawn largely from Quebec, Montreal, Trois Rivères, and small hamlets along the St. Lawrence River.

No one could miss a voyageur. They wore bright clothes that were a mix of Native American and European styles: red caps, beaded shirts and moccasins, leather leggings that extended from the ankles to just above the knees, and breech cloths. As writer Grace Lee Nute described:

> One would expect the voyageurs to be men of heroic proportions, but usually they were not. The average voyageur was five feet six inches in height. Few were more than five feet eight inches. Had they been taller, they would have occupied too much of the precious space in a canoe already overcrowded with cargo. But though the voyageur was short, he was strong. He could paddle fifteen—yes, if necessary, eighteen—hours per day for weeks on end and joke beside the camp fire at the close of each day's toil. He could carry from 200 to 450 pounds of merchandise on his back over rocky portage trails at a pace which made unburdened travelers pant for breath in their endeavor not to be left behind. A distinguished traveler on the Great Lakes in 1828... wrote how his men took the canoe out of the water, mended a breach in it, reloaded, cooked breakfast, shaved, washed, ate, and reëmbarked—all in *fifty-seven* minutes!

Packed with trade goods, the voyageurs maneuvered seemingly fragile birch-bark canoes across the Great Lakes, even into the treacherous open waters of Lake Superior, to Grand Portage. If they were going further still, they would unpack their vessels and portage them as well as their contents in relays nine miles through the wilderness to the next navigable water and then on westward. The canoes themselves were modified from native designs and ranged from the great forty-foot Montreal Canoes to smaller twenty-five-foot North Canoes. A simple wood frame was covered with birch and sealed with pine-resin pitch to make these crafts. A rock or a piece of driftwood could easily put a hole in the bottom, and voyageurs who carried passengers preferred—often to their passenger's dismay—to lift their charges bodily out of the canoe

Must-See Sites: North West Company Fur Post, Pine City

The North West Company Fur Post and an Ojibwe wigwam helps visitors envision the era of fur trade and the voyageurs. Costumed guides introduce visitors to the era. A fur trade clerk might explain the system of barter that moved beaver fur from the hands of Native American hunters onto the heads of fashionable Europeans. An Ojibwe woman may explain how her band's seasonal industries changed when Europeans arrived. The post has been reconstructed on its original 1804 site and has a variety of heritage trails to explore. A new Visitors Center features a retail shop and modern amenities, with an exhibits hall scheduled to open in the spring of 2003. Guided tours of the historic site are offered, including to a relocated Ojibwe encampment.

Contact: (320) 629-6356; E-mail: nwcfurpost@mnhs.org; Web: www.mnhs.org

Location: 1.5 miles west of I-35 at exit 169 (Pine County Highway 7), Pine City.

and carry them on their backs to shore rather than risk beaching a loaded vessel. Though it was easily damaged, the birch-bark canoe was also easily repaired with materials that could be carried or found along the way. Each canoe was brightly painted with designs and lettering.

In the center of the canoe (aside from any passengers) were the middlemen, the main engines, who provided the motive power for the vessel. In the rear sat the gouvernail or helmsman who steered the canoe with a longer paddle. At the front, with the largest paddle, was the bowsman whose skill came in handy when the laden canoe shot the white water rapids or leapt small waterfalls.

An early passenger, Robert Kennicott, wrote: "All, except the steersman, keep perfect stroke in paddling." The voyageurs, he continued, "paddle with great rapidity making forty strokes per minute… dipping the paddle a foot or eighteen inches into the water and pulling with very considerable force." Other travelers reported canoemen who could manage a stroke a second. With the help of a small sail and favorable wind, the canoes could reach ten miles an hour, though four to six was more common. The voyageurs could travel this way, with short rest breaks, for a long as eighteen hours a day, and it is little wonder that they achieved mythic status in the eyes of later observers. To the voyageurs themselves, such endurance was a point of pride, and weakness was a thing to be mocked. Said one aged former canoeman: "I could paddle, walk, and sing with any man I ever saw. I have been twenty-four years a canoeman, and forty-one in service; no portage was ever too long for me. Fifty songs I could sing. I have saved the lives of ten voyageurs. Have had twelve wives and six running dogs. I spent all my money in pleasure. Were I young again, I should spend my life the same way over."

Along the way, to pass the time and to keep a steady stroke, they sang. They sang chanties, dancing songs, bawdy songs, drinking songs, love songs, religious songs, songs of people journeying far from home. The words to "Petit Rocher" (or "Little Rock") went:

> O little rock of the mountain I stand on,
> I venture here my campaign to abandon.
>   Ah! Echoes sweet, give ear to unto my sigh,
>   Languid with wounds I come here to die. . . .
>
> Say, nightingale, to the wife I'm bereaving,
> Just an adieu to my children I'm leaving,
>   Still I have kept my love and loyalty,
>   And from this time she must give up hope of me.

The verses to voyageur songs went on and on, because short songs were no good for long distances. The tunes were drawn from contemporary French or English folk songs and the lyrics (often in unlettered French) came mostly from Gascony, Normandy, Picardy, or Flanders, often modified or reinvented to suit local conditions.

Expeditions set out in the spring as soon as the weather permitted. The traders might stop along the way at Native American villages to trade or stock up on supplies, or at some well-known camps or portages where friends might leave messages for each other. On reaching Grand Portage, some expeditions might continue further to the Rainy River and Lake of the Woods. There, they might meet the elite voyageurs who had spent the winter in the wilderness, even as far west as the Columbia River. These voyageurs would have collected furs from Native Americans in the far reaches of the north country and relayed them to the expeditions and in turn received resupply and a new stock of trade goods. The furs would be brought to outposts like Grand Portage, where they would be recorded, packed into canoes for transshipment further east and eventually to the east coast or Europe.

Furs poured in throughout the short northern summer, carried on the backs of voyageurs. By the time of the American Revolution, the yearly fur trade at Grand Portage was worth an estimated 40,000 pounds sterling. By then, control of the trade was in the hands of the Northwest Company, based in Montreal and staffed by a mixture of French Canadians, Scots, and English. Small ships were used to transport furs and trade goods across the lakes to and from eastern depots, but the voyageurs were still needed to carry the furs to the posts and carry trade goods back to the native peoples.

Although this backwoods commerce may have seemed remote from the larger world, the fur trade was Minnesota's first encounter with globalization (which is hardly a new concept anyway). Demand for fur was stimulated by the fashions of Europe. In turn, goods flowed into Minnesota from around the world: vermilion from China, glass beads from Venice and Bohemia, tobacco from Brazil, rum from the West Indies, steel knives from Sheffield in the English Midlands, wool blankets from Flemish and British textile mills.

During the height of the trading season, Grand Portage bustled with activity, color, and life. There one could hear Ojibwe and other Algonquin dialects, French in varying forms, and, increasingly after 1763, English spoken with British, Scottish, and American accents. Native American quill work and bright European fabrics contrasted with drab woolen wear and buckskin or the dark robes of Jesuit priests. Stray dogs roamed the muddy grounds searching for scraps of food. Wintering voyageurs arrived to trade for fresh supplies, to drink, dance, and party. "Marriages" with local Native American and mixed-race women "by the custom of the country" were common and sometimes quite brief.

The custom of French men marrying Native American women was common throughout the Great Lakes. Later English, Scottish, and American traders also married Native American women, but apparently did not intermingle to the same extent as the French. Whether this was due to a greater shortage of French women in the New World, or the fact that the French were the first Europeans to reach many tribes, or simply some closer cultural connection between the two is not clear. Native American women were considered highly desirable as wives, especially for men who were far from home and often desperately lonely. Even more so were mixed-race women. Travelers in the region were often stunned by the "classical beauty" of these women. According to author Joseph Kinsey Howard, they were considered "gay companions, industrious helpmeets, affectionate wives, and devoted mothers." For the women, traders represented a rise in status, as the traders were not merely wealthy but also industrious men. By marrying outside their immediate surroundings, these young women also gained a greater measure of freedom from traditional obligations. Ojibwe, Cree, and later Dakota women, by marrying with the newcomers, created a bridge of blood and kinship that allowed both groups to live and interact with each other in a more or less peaceful fashion. In cases where marriages were temporary, some of the children stayed with their mother's people while others were adopted into French-Canadian communities.

Very often, intense bonds of love kept these interracial marriages together, and this resulted not only in many Europeans living in native villages, but the creation of a whole new people. By 1800 there were an estimated 30,000 mixed race people scattered from northern Minnesota and south-central Canada to the Rocky Mountains. They did not fully fit into either Native American or European-stock cultures and they developed their own identity as a people and their own name: the Métis (which in French means "mixed"). Métis historian Nicholas Vrooman wrote:

> The Métis prided themselves on having the best of both worlds. Their European-style clothing was adorned in Indian fashion, often blending beadwork and tartan, symbols of their tribal and clan heritage. For entertainment they played the fiddle but employed a drum rhythm, and they danced the jig in an Indian manner. Deeply religious, they prayed to Jesus, yet sang medicine songs of healing…. In the retelling of medieval European fairy tales they introduced a native cast of characters…. From their two heritages, they created a new language—Michif—a beautiful blending of French nouns and Indian verbs.

The original Métis homeland encompassed much of northwest Minnesota, northeast North Dakota, the southern half of Manitoba, and parts of Saskatchewan. Its heart was Pembina, settled in 1780, at the point where the Red River meets the 48th parallel, or today's U.S.–Canadian border. As the great era of the canoe-laden voyageurs came to an end, the Métis took center stage.

At the start of the nineteenth century, as the source of the fur trade shifted further west and north, the Métis held the position of middlemen. To the north was the Hudson's Bay Company (which would later merge with its Montreal rival the Northwestern Company). To the south were the new American outposts, particularly St. Paul. The Métis gathered or traded for furs from afar and carried them to Pembina, where they could be sent south by means of a simple horse-drawn wooden cart, called the Red River cart.

Like their voyageur forbearers, the Red River cartmen faced great hardship and difficulty, as Joseph Howard related:

Wind-borne swarms of mosquitoes, often preceding thunderstorms, bore down on the cart brigades in such numbers that horses, dogs and drivers were overwhelmed in seconds. While the horses pitched and screamed under the attack of the savage insects and the dogs writhed in agony on the ground, the men fled under their carts and wound themselves, head to foot, in blankets, though the temperature might be in the nineties. The torment might only last a few minutes, but it frequently killed horses and dogs and disabled the men for days.

Sometimes the approaching swarms could be heard: a high, unbroken and terrifying hum. This gave the drivers time to throw wagon sheets over their animals. Mounted men would attempt to outrun the flying horde. Though they were almost always overtaken, the breeze created by their horses' panic flight saved them from the worst agony; but they pulled out of the gallop, miles way, with faces and arms streaming blood and with the insects six deep on their ponies.

AMERICAN RULE

After the American Revolution, the British ceded their portion of what is now Minnesota to the new United States in 1783. The land west of the Mississippi had been ceded to Spain by France, but there was no effective Spanish influence in the area. The British remained the dominant commercial power through the influence of the two rival trading companies. By 1800 these companies had established trading posts all across Minnesota, along all of the major rivers and many minor ones as well. This continued even after a treaty in 1794 was signed to secure American boundaries. In 1800, as Napoleon's power in Europe grew, Spain ceded the vast Louisiana territory to France. The French, however, realized that it was impossible to hold this land in the face of the British navy and in 1803 sold it to the United States, bringing all of the modern territory of Minnesota under the American flag (at least officially).

During this early period of American rule, there was not much practical control over the region and things changed but little. Away in Washington, however, the U.S. Congress passed the Northwest Ordinance in 1787, which would have important consequences for the future Minnesota. The law stipulated that this territory was to be divided into three to five districts, which could attain first territorial status and eventually become states of the Union. This principle was to govern all future land acquisitions by the United States. Furthermore, the act stipulated that in these northwestern lands, slavery and involuntary servitude were prohibited.

The fur trade was still the dominant commercial activity, and the region's Métis and Native American inhabitants were unconcerned with the fact that their homeland now straddled two countries. As the fur trade moved west, following the remaining available fur-bearing animals, the British companies faced an increasing disadvantage. American traders had ready access to the territory via the Mississippi River. In fact, until the completion of the Canadian Pacific Railway in 1885, travel between eastern Canada and Manitoba was easiest through St. Paul. Furthermore, the Americans paid more for furs and gave better deals on manufactured goods. The American influence worried British officials and cut into revenue. Efforts to settle Europeans in Manitoba sparked resistance from local Métis and backfired due to internal rivalries.

Although the Americans were not able to exercise immediate control over the territory that would become Minnesota, both the government and the public became aware of the possibilities of this vast new land. In 1804 President Thomas Jefferson authorized the Lewis and Clark expedition to follow the Missouri into the Pacific and Oregon Territory. Even before that expedition returned, however, a second expedition was ordered north to explore the upper Mississippi basin. In command was twenty-five-year-old First Lieutenant Zebulon M. Pike.

Setting out in August 1805, Pike's orders were to map the land, make contact with local Native Americans, and find suitable locations for the siting of government forts and trading posts. By September, he and his men had reached the confluence of the Minnesota and Mississippi Rivers. There, Pike met a band of about 150 Dakota warriors. After gift giving and some speeches, Pike managed to convince the leaders of the band to sign a treaty on behalf of the "Sioux nation" allowing the U.S. to establish military posts in the region, giving the Americans a swath of land at the meeting points of the Mississippi, Minnesota, and St. Croix Rivers. Article two, which was to stipulate what the U.S. gave the Sioux in return, was left blank and only later filled in by the

U.S. Senate when it ratified the treaty in 1808. (They filled in the amount of $2,000.)

From a legal standpoint, Pike's treaty was nonsense. Neither Pike nor the Native Americans who signed were authorized to make such treaties. Native chiefs, as we have seen, had relatively little ability to command followers in the sense of military commanders. Nor did they have the authority to give away land that, as the Native Americans saw it, was not something to be sold. There is little doubt that what was to happen to the Native Americans of the Upper Midwest over the course of the next century would have happened without the signing of any treaties. Yet such treaties made it easier to justify mistreatment and dispossession of native peoples.

Pike then proceeded to Little Falls and to Upper Red Cedar Lake, which he proclaimed to be the source of the Mississippi. Along the way, Pike tried to be a diplomat representing the United States, though we may imagine the reaction of the people he met. He paid visits at two Northwest Company posts, where he was feted, but where he discovered, to his irritation, that they were still flying the Union Jack in violation of the 1783 treaty. On one occasion, Pike had his men shoot the British flag down from the flag pole. He informed the traders that they needed to first pay duties on all goods sold at Mackinac, Michigan (the approved border crossing), to conform to all U.S. laws, have no political dealings with the Native Americans, and not to fly the British flag. In his encounters with the Ojibwe, Pike demanded they return all medals and flags given to them as gifts by the British, that they pay all outstanding debts, and that they were now under the rule of the "Great Father" in Washington. This did not win Pike or the U.S. government many friends.

During the War of 1812, the British quickly reasserted control over the entire region. Local Native Americans from Minnesota and Wisconsin favored the British over the less tractable Americans and this allowed the British to capture Prairie du Chien on today's Iowa–Wisconsin border. British influence via the fur companies remained until after the founding of Fort Snelling in 1820. (One northern Minnesota Ojibwe family retained a British flag, given to them in friendship during this period, passing it down through the generations until 1979 when it was donated to the state historical society.)

Fort Snelling, 1865

Concern over continuing British influence in the region and plans by a Hudson's Bay Company official, the Earl of Selkirk, to start an agricultural colony in what is now southern Manitoba drove the Americans to send additional expeditions into Minnesota following the end of the War of 1812. In 1820 an American military expedition under the command of Colonel Josiah Snelling began construction of a fort atop the bluffs overlooking the meeting point of the Minnesota and Mississippi River. Unlike previous forts founded in the region since the late 1600s, which had been built of wood, Snelling built a massive stone edifice suited to repel even an attack by a conventional European army. The diamond-shaped enclosure, constructed of local limestone, was strengthened

Must-See Sites: Fort Snelling, St. Paul

This well-preserved 1820s military outpost was once a distant outpost of the early American republic. The settlement that grew up around it became Minnesota's Twin Cities metropolitan area. The restored stone fortress welcomes visitors to a glimpse of frontier life complete with guides in full costume, circa the late 1820s. A company of soldiers performs drills and practices firing musket and cannon. Other interpreters show off the fort's everyday life: mending clothes, cooking food, or scraping hides. The fort's costumed guides conduct tours, demonstrate crafts, present historical skits, and practice military drill and weapons firings. Join them in 1827 or explore other areas of the site's long history in the exhibits.

Contact: (612) 726-1171; E-mail: ftsnelling@mnhs.org; Web: www.mnhs.org

Location: At the junction of Minnesota Highways 5 and 55, one mile east of the Twin Cities International Airport, St. Paul.

by towers and gun emplacements. Completed in 1825, it was named after its builder as Fort Snelling. The new fortress was the key that locked up the Northwest Territory for the young American Republic.

What exactly had been locked up, however, was not entirely clear to the Americans. Pike's expedition and earlier French and British efforts had yielded important information, but maps were rudimentary and careful land surveys were lacking for most of the state. Moreover, many people doubted that Pike had actually found the source of the Mississippi River. To truly gain control of Minnesota, the Americans needed to map and record what was there and who was there.

Lewis Cass, governor of the Michigan Territory, led an expedition in search of the Mississippi's source in 1820. Like Pike, he concluded that Upper Red Cedar Lake (today named Cass Lake) was the source of the great river. Cass brought with him a geologist named Henry Rowe Schoolcraft whose own reports made clear that he doubted Cass and Pike's conclusion. In 1832, Schoolcraft returned to the region. Having mastered the Ojibwe language with the help of his mixed-race wife, Schoolcraft secured the help of the native people who knew the region best. With a local Native American guide, Schoolcraft found a lake the Ojibwe called Elk Lake (due to its shape, which looked like an elk's antlers). Schoolcraft, however, christened it Lake Itasca by amalgamating Latin and Ojibwe words. This proved to be the source for the Father of Waters.

Frenchman Joseph Nicollet followed Schoolcraft a few years later and made accurate maps of the Itasca region. He and future presidential candidate John C. Frémont later returned with a government expedition that mapped large portions of the state and named many geographical features. Nicollet provided the first accurate map of the state and the first significant description of its features and resources.

By the 1820s, the Americans dominated Minnesota and its fur trade. John Jacob Astor's American Fur Company established itself at Mendota and though it was challenged by serious rivals, it remained the most important player in the trade. In addition to furs brought from Canada by the Métis, local muskrat pelts became an important trade item. Thus, the fur trade and its outposts spread out from the forests of the north, even to the smaller streams and lakes of the prairie region.

The American takeover, however, was not the continuation of the old fur trade under a new flag. When the British took over from the French, they had largely maintained the system of mutual accommodation worked out between Native Americans and Europeans. Aside from a few key forts, the fur trade did not require either Britain or France to commit large garrisons of troops to secure northern America. Instead, both powers relied on a shifting set of alliances with the tribes, reinforced by gift giving, trade, intermarriage, and tokens of friendship. This system—like any human creation—had its flaws and it often broke down. Yet it suited both sides fairly well.

Britain's own American colonists, however, were another matter. As poor people (some former indentured servants) seeking their own farms or simply wanting to be free from the constraints of government, colonists sought land to settle. That meant Native American land. Early on, colonial governments realized that this was a major problem for the Native Americans and could upset the alliances that secured the lucrative fur trade. The colonists, however, did not care about a trade from which they saw little benefit. The tribes, of course, were enraged to lose their land, for the colonists were not merely settlers but were often tough frontiersmen capable of facing the Native Americans on their own terms. Conflicts resulted in bloodshed on both sides and bloodshed led to cycles of revenge killing. Unlike the Native Americans, however, the colonists could not be subsumed into the system of gift giving, which was how British and French leaders had been able to make peace. When colonists lost family or neighbors, they demanded European-style justice that was culturally alien to the Native Americans. Prior to the Revolutionary War, the British had tried to restrict settlement on Native American land, but after their defeat, American settlers moved west in increasing numbers. A series of "Indian Wars" and forced expulsions began to drive the native peoples west. This caused a hardening of attitudes on all sides. The Americans had a far less subtle face; although they did at times distribute various tokens of friendship, they were far more likely to make what Native Americans considered harsh demands and to threaten with force. In addition, the Americans devised a long series of treaties with Native Americans that resulted in the the loss of their land in exchange for promises that were rarely honored.

As they entered Minnesota, American officials assigned to work with the native tribes, already at a disadvantage, found themselves among people with a long and complex history. The most immediate problem was the continuous conflict between the Ojibwe and the Dakota. As in the past, both groups looked to the Americans to arbitrate the dispute and provide a settlement. Unlike the British, however, the Americans tried to impose a European-style settlement by drawing a boundary line to divide the tribes. Such lines made little sense to people who had never seen a map and who were accustomed to move about as they pleased. So the conflict continued.

In the 1840s, the Americans tried an even more ham-handed effort at peacemaking. As neighboring Wisconsin became a focus for increasing settlement, its tribes had often been pushed out. The Ho-Chunk people lived in central and western Wisconsin and tried to cling to their homeland. The government uprooted them, moved them to central Minnesota, and tried to make them into a buffer between the warring Ojibwe and Dakota. Although they spoke a language more closely related to Dakota, the Ho-Chunk were not especially friendly with either tribe. As a result, the Ho-Chunk were attacked by both sides. They were then relocated to a new reservation just south of the Minnesota River and later to Iowa.

As American settlers came to the region in ever-greater numbers, as the fur trade declined in relative economic significance, and as the Native Americans felt ever more embattled and threatened, policy mistakes and bad treaties compounded and resentments increased. The result would be death and tragedy for both Native Americans and settlers.

4

TERRITORY AND STATE: 1820–1860

With the completion of Fort Snelling (originally called Fort St. Anthony), the United States confirmed its control over the upper reaches of the Mississippi. Although the general outlines were known to the Americans, much of the region that would become Minnesota was not. Its population, not counting the fort's garrison, consisted mostly of Native Americans, Métis, and few European traders. Aside from a few isolated trading posts, American culture in the 1820s was confined to the fort itself.

The people at the fort remained fairly isolated, although the first steam-powered vessel, the *Virginia*, reached the outpost from St. Louis in 1823. In addition to working on the fort and its buildings, and the usual military drill, the men of the 5th U.S. Infantry stationed in Minnesota spent much of their time engaged in agriculture, planting crops and tending cattle that grazed free along the river. This was essential, since regular supplies could not be counted on, especially over the winter when the rivers froze.

The fort itself, aside from its walls, towers, and parade ground, contained living space for officers and men, a magazine (where the powder and arms were kept), a hospital, guardhouse, and stores for supplies. It was a fairly cramped position, though highly secure. Outside the walls were a bakehouse, boat landing, wash house, cemetery, and gardens.

In addition to the officers and men, a few of the officers, including its commander, Josiah Snelling, brought their wives and children, therefore establishing what could be called the true start of American settlement. Few civilians settled in the area, although a couple German-Swiss families joined the community, arriving after the failure of the Selkirk colony in Manitoba. In addition to soldiers, government officials, traders, and the odd settler or two, a trickle of Protestant missionaries, usually funded by Bible societies and churches in New England or New York, came to spread the word of God among the "heathen."

In general, life at the fort was tough. Although the physical hardships of the first years were mitigated once the fort's buildings were completed in 1825, perhaps the greatest enemies faced by the average soldiers were loneliness, homesickness, and boredom. Cheap liquor was freely available and resulted in high rates of alcohol abuse. In addition, mail and pay were often delayed thanks to inconstant boat service between the fort and St. Louis. Early records show bounties were frequently paid to those who found and returned deserters, who often went AWOL in groups of as many as half a dozen. As in any small community, personality conflicts loomed large and the fort's first commander was himself prone to drink and frequently abused his subordinates, a fact that contributed to his transfer in 1827. (His position was given to future president Zachary Taylor, who served only one year.)

A school for the children living in and around the fort was open intermittently by the late 1830s. One itinerant teacher, Peter Garrioch, had a low opinion of his charges. In 1837 he wrote:

> Opened my school on the heterogeneous system. The whole number of brats who attended for the purpose of being benefited by my notions… amounted to thirty. The number is composed of English, French, Swiss, Cree, Chippewa, Sioux and Negro extraction. Such a composition and such a group of geniuses, I never saw before. May it never be my privilege to meet another.

Although we may wonder what sort of teacher he was, his words provide a picture of the great diversity of the area's population even at that early stage.

Among those stationed at the fort was a Doctor John Emerson. Emerson owned a slave named Dred Scott, who, after his master's death, sued to gain his freedom due to having lived in Minnesota, a free territory where slavery was illegal. When the U.S. Supreme Court denied Scott's bid, it essentially struck down the Missouri Compromise that had accepted states into the Union in a careful balance, one slave state for each free state. By saying that Scott could be held as a slave in a free state, the court seemed to be allowing slavery in all states, a decision that set off a chain of events that led to the Civil War.

The occasional visitor to the fort provided interesting diversions. One of these was an adventuresome Italian count, Giacomo Beltrami, who arrived aboard the *Virginia* in 1823 and stayed with the Snelling family for a few months, tutoring their daughter in French and hunting in the nearby wilds. Josiah Snelling's son Henry recalled that Beltrami rode up and attacked a bull bison with a knife. Chased by the enraged beast, Beltrami led the animal toward a companion who shot the bison:

> This brought [the bison] to his knees, and the Count springing from the saddle attacked him with his knife. His impetuosity nearly proved fatal to the Count, for the beast, although mortally wounded was not yet vanquished, and summoning all his strength, he made a violent plunge at the Count and sent him reeling some distance. At this juncture Mr. S—— came up and again discharging his piece, the ball passed through the noble creature's heart and put an end to his struggles.

Aside from such escapades, the fort's residents often interacted with the local native population and it was not uncommon for single officers to take up with local Native American or mixed-race women, a practice that became less common as more and more American women migrated to the state. The establishment of such permanent settlements deepened the racial gulf.

Racial differences were exacerbated by cultural and religious differences. The Native American and mixed-race population had for the most part been catechized by French missionaries. Even if they maintained only the thinnest veneer of Christianity, many had adopted some of the jollier Catholic practices, such as the celebration of Christmas. The earlier missionaries and officials often came from the New England states where Christmas celebrations had at times been illegal and was at best viewed as a Papist superstition if not outright heresy. William Boutwell, an American missionary at Leech Lake in the early 1830s, recorded his disgust with local Christmas and New Year's customs:

Must-See Sites: Split Rock Lighthouse/Gooseberry Falls State Park, Two Harbors

Shipwrecks from a 1905 November gale prompted the construction of the Split Rock Lighthouse. Completed by the U.S. Lighthouse Service in 1910, Split Rock Light Station was soon one of Minnesota's best-known landmarks. Restored to its 1920s appearance, the lighthouse offers a glimpse of lighthouse life in this remote and spectacular setting. Tour the lighthouse, fog-signal building, and restored keeper's dwelling. A visitor center features an award-winning film, exhibits, and a museum store.

Nearby Gooseberry Falls State Park is the gateway to the North Shore. It is known for its spectacular waterfalls, river gorge, Lake Superior shoreline, Civilian Conservation Corps log and stone structures, and north woods wildlife. Visitors can listen to the thunderous roar of the upper, middle, and lower falls of the Gooseberry River as it plummets through a rocky gorge, or watch waves, ships, or a moonrise on Lake Superior from the ancient lava of the Picnic Flow. The park offers hiking or skiing through a forest of evergreen, aspen, and birch, as well as camping, picnicking, and trout fishing from the Lake Superior shoreline or the Gooseberry River.

Contact (Split Rock): (218) 226-6372; E-mail: splitrock@mnhs.org

Contact (Gooseberry Falls): (218) 834-3855; Web: www.dnr.state.mn.us/state_parks/ or www.stayatmnparks.com

Location: Split Rock Lighthouse State Park is on Hwy 61, 20 miles northeast of Two Harbors. Gooseberry Falls State Park is approximately 13 miles northeast of Two Harbors on Highway 61.

Open came our door, and in came 5 or 6 women and as many children. An old squaw, with clean face, for once, came and saluted me with, "bon jour," giving her hand at the same time, which I received, returning her compliment, "bon jour." But this was not all. She had been too long among [French] Canadians not to learn some of their New Year's customs. She approached— approached so near, to give and receive a kiss, that I was obliged to give her a slip, and dodge! This vexed the old lady and provoked her to say, that I thought her too dirty. But pleased or displeased, I was determined to give no countenance to a custom which I hated more than dirt.

Most of the state's inhabitants were Native Americans. By the time Minnesota became an official territory in 1849, it had an officially surveyed Native American population of over 31,000 (which included people of mixed race living like Native Americans or with Native Americans). This was five times the size of the white population. The official estimate included over 20,000 Dakota, with about 3,500 Ojibwe, 2,500 Ho-Chunk, and smaller numbers of Hidatsa, Arikara, and Mandan. These numbers were probably minimal since most Ojibwe lived in areas of the state that were not easily accessible.

At that time, United States Native American policy varied between paternalism, neglect, hostility, and in extreme cases, a desire to kill or remove native peoples. In 1819 Lawrence Taliafero (pronounced "Toliver") was appointed U.S. Indian agent at Fort Snelling. Taliafero was a rare agent in that he seems to have genuinely cared about the Native Americans and did not seek to cheat them. He struggled to restrain the trade in liquor and to ensure that the Native Americans were given what they had been promised.

The agent fought against almost impossible odds to do his job and often despaired: "The time would come," he wrote, "when all my efforts to do good would pass into oblivion and the nationality of the noble Sioux be completely destroyed." In 1839, Taliafero finally resigned, writing: "I am disgusted with the life of an Agent among such bad materials and bad management on the part of Congress—The Indian Office etc., etc.... I have the Sad Consolation of leaving... the public service as poor as when I first entered it... the only evidence of my integrity."

Taliafero's experience not withstanding, the post of Indian agent was usually a coveted political perk because it allowed a man to get rich. As Native American lands were taken in exchange for yearly annuity, the agents were in charge of doling out the payments. In addition to simply stealing from the Native Americans, agents could also make money on commissions and through deals with traders. Native Americans were given credit for food and goods throughout the year at vastly inflated prices. Thus the annuity payments went first to pay off these debts. The net effect was to reduce many Native Americans to debt peonage.

TREATIES AND THE ROAD TO STATEHOOD

The first major land treaty came in 1837. Up until that time, only small parts of the state were officially open to settlement or under the control of the U.S. government. In 1837, with eastern timber interests eyeing the region's stands of hardwood, the government negotiated a treaty with the Ojibwe in which they gave up all land between the Mississippi and St. Croix rivers for seven cents an acre and the right to continue hunting, ricing, and fishing on the land. The Dakota, too, were persuaded to give up their land east of the Mississippi.

The coming of American timber interests to Minnesota also signaled the decline of the fur trade in relative economic importance. The 1820s and 1830s saw a continuance of the trade under American domination. Many of the state's first political leaders grew wealthy on the trade but shifted their interests elsewhere. Fort Snelling and St. Paul continued their importance as a collection point for fur coming down from British territory well into the 1850s, but by then the richest furs from Minnesota were long gone.

Minnesota's road to statehood and the determination of its boundaries were bound up with national politics. The Northwest Ordinance had stipulated that states formed out of this territory would be free states, but until the U.S.–Mexican War settlement, statehood beyond the Mississippi was considered a somewhat unlikely notion. With the acquisition of Texas, New Mexico, and California, as well as the Oregon Territory, the United States became a continental power, and the notion of a swath of states

stretching across North America was suddenly not so
farfetched. American expansionists, such as Stephen
Douglas of Illinois, who also opposed slavery, saw in the
northwest an opportunity to create free states, linked to
eastern interests that would counteract the addition of
states like Texas and Arkansas. With Michigan organized
as a state in 1837, Iowa followed suit in 1846 and Wisconsin
in 1848. Each state's boundary was set by a series of political
compromises. Douglas, in particular, limited Wisconsin's
western border to the line of the St. Croix and Mississippi
with an eye toward creating another state. Prior to
Wisconsin statehood, however, much of Minnesota had
been designated as part of Wisconsin Territory. In 1848, the
land west of Wisconsin became no-man's-land, but not for
long. Local leaders of what was then a thinly populated
area gathered together in Stillwater in 1848 to ask that the
government create a new territory out of the now
unorganized land that had not been included as part of
either Iowa or Wisconsin. As Minnesota historian
Theodore Blegen related: "Some ingenuous soul now came
up with the idea that the Territory of Wisconsin was still in
existence and that it consisted of the part of the territory
that had been left out of the state of Wisconsin!"

As a result, self-constituted and with a self-declared
governor, a group of Minnesotans from "Wisconsin
Territory" elected fur trader Henry Sibley as their delegate to
Washington. He went to the nation's capitol and, with as
much *sang froid* as a fur trader could muster, managed to
convince the House of Representatives to seat him as the
representative of Wisconsin Territory. With the urging of the
audacious Sibley, the sponsorship of Sen. Douglas, and plenty
of political wrangling, Congress approved a bill to create
Minnesota Territory, which became law in March 1849.

The boundaries of the new territory were already set
on its eastern, southern, and northern sides. To the west,
however, Minnesota Territory extended all the way to the
Missouri River, taking in much of today's states of North
and South Dakota. Only a fraction of the land included in
this new territory was legally open to settlement. Even the
area that was officially open was sparsely populated. Yet
within this area the kernel of a number of towns had
already begun.

The first settlers had clustered in the small military reservation around Fort Snelling, but as time went on the fort's commanders grew concerned about the depletion of timber around the fort and in 1840 forced the settlers to relocate and leveled their small cabins. Therefore, the fort itself never became the nucleus for settlement. These settlers moved slightly downriver to the east. Legend has it that the land they took up was owned by a French-Canadian dealer in illegal liquor called Pete "Pig's Eye" Parrant who operated out of caves in the bluffs above the river. Although the early settlement was known as Pig's Eye, it was later christened St. Paul. (A local lake, however, still bears Parrant's nickname.) The early inhabitants were primarily French Canadian, Swiss, and some Yankees. With its relatively large Catholic population, St. Paul also became the logical place for a Catholic mission and, in 1851, of a new diocese to serve the territory. By 1849, the town was the largest in the new territory and thus also the logical place for the capital of the territory. State government and Catholicism would help give the city its character.

Early St. Paul, like many of Minnesota's towns after their founding, was a boom town. As a river-oriented city, settlement spread first along the banks of the Mississippi and then inland. Buildings sprang up seemingly overnight. Each summer St. Paul's population swelled as landseekers, merchants, and travelers took advantage of steamboats running from St. Louis. In 1849 a traveler there listed among the town's resources two hotels, government offices, stores, saloons, a public school (run by a young woman from New England), a Catholic church, four other ministers, three printing houses, and a bank that issued its own notes. By then, the city had become home to the territory's first newspaper, the *Minnesota Pioneer*.

Upriver from Fort Snelling, a rather different community was forming. The Falls of St. Anthony had long been recognized as a potential source of waterpower for industrial applications and caused both Iowa and Wisconsin politicians to cast covetous eyes in its direction. The U.S. army had also understood the economic potential of the falls and built a small grist mill at the site in the early 1820s to produce flour to feed the soldiers at the fort.

Following the 1837 treaty with the Ojibwe, speculators bought up land around the river and the falls in the hopes of building a saw mill that would process logs to be floated down the Mississippi. It took several years, but in 1847 a dam and mill were built. In 1849, the city of St. Anthony was founded on the east side of the Mississippi. On the west side of the river, Minneapolis got a slightly slower start but was founded in 1852. In time, this city would overshadow and absorb the slightly older St. Anthony.

The state's first lumber boom, however, occurred on the St. Croix River. North of St. Paul, the small communities of Stillwater and Marine-on-St.-Croix got their start when saw mills opened there as early as 1839. Close to Wisconsin, the rivers, and the new territorial capital, Stillwater grew quickly. In 1849 it was second only to St. Paul in population, though Stillwater had a mere 609 residents.

To the south of St. Paul, along the Mississippi, a string of river towns were founded based on the steam boat, including Red Wing (1850), Winona (1852), and Hastings (1855). To the south, along the Minnesota River, St. Peter was founded in 1853. To the north on the Mississippi, St. Cloud was founded in three parts between 1853 and 1855. Most of these early river towns appeared at sites that had been first occupied as fur trading posts.

The settlement of so many towns, not to mention the farmland in between, would not have been possible without taking more land from Minnesota's native peoples. In this respect, territorial status was a losing proposition for the Native Americans, since the creation of the territorial leadership meant the creation of a group of people with a vested interest in expanding the land available for American settlement. The ultimate goal of these leaders was to make Minnesota a state, which could only be done if the population increased, and the population could only increase enough through in-migration and that required the lure of cheap and productive land. In any case, legal prohibitions had never stopped Americans on the frontier from moving into Native American territory, and no matter what the government had to say about such violations, good or bad, it rarely had the power or desire to police a vast land with a sparse population.

Still, squatters were no use to territorial leaders seeking a population they could legally count, and for the first two years they lobbied the U.S. Congress to purchase more land from the Native Americans. Supporting Minnesota's local interests were expansionists in Congress and elsewhere for whom Manifest Destiny was more than just a slogan. Naturally, the Native American leaders were reluctant to sell their land, even though they could plainly see what was happening. Nevertheless, their position was often undercut, in what would become an all-too-familiar "family feud," by the mixed-race families who often stood to gain in any deals between whites and Native Americans. In addition, many well-meaning whites who genuinely cared about the Native Americans, though in a paternalistic way, counseled them to give up their old ways and accept the treaties. Finally, there were also plenty of unscrupulous people willing to take advantage of the Native Americans, or the government, or both to make a buck.

In 1851 the government negotiated a major land treaty with the Dakota. Recognizing the writing on the wall, Dakota leaders agreed to give up virtually all of their land west of the Mississippi, constituting the southern two thirds of modern-day Minnesota. They retained a reservation of the land they loved the most: the Minnesota River valley northwest of what is now New Ulm. And they were to receive yearly cash payments and even help if they wanted to learn American-style farming. On paper, it was probably the best deal they could have hoped for, but deals on paper are often different from the reality.

In 1854 and again in 1855, the U.S. negotiated further treaties with the Ojibwe in northern and central Minnesota. The Ojibwe gave up nearly all of northeastern and north-central Minnesota, retaining a series of scattered reservations and leaving most of northwest Minnesota unceded. Meanwhile, the unfortunate Ho-Chunk were moved once again. In 1855 they gave up their "reservation" in central Minnesota (part of which they had never really occupied) and were moved to a smaller reservation in south-central Minnesota. In less than five years, virtually the entire present-day state of Minnesota was taken from the Native Americans and opened to settlement.

The first white settlers of New Ulm, 1854

MINNESOTA TERRITORY

In 1850, the 6,077 official—that is, non-Native American, non-squatter—residents of Minnesota Territory were made up mostly of native-born Americans. About four in ten were born in another state and about one in four were born in Minnesota. Just about one in three had been born outside of the U.S. As was typical with a pioneer state, men outnumbered women three to two. There was a tiny free African American population of 21 men and 18 women, the majority being classified by the census as "mulattoes" or people of mixed race. Reflecting the importance and attraction of the early timber industry, the heaviest concentration of people was recorded in Washington County, the area around Stillwater between St. Paul and the Wisconsin border.

Within ten years, Minnesota's population had increased by 28 times, to 172,023. The number of dwellings recorded

by the census grew by over 40 times in that same period. The biggest group of newcomers were Yankees, people from New England or with origins in New England. From the end of the Revolution, these Americans had been migrating westward across the northern tier of states: first to New York, then to the Great Lakes states, and finally to Minnesota Territory.

During that era, Yankees were viewed as a type: They were hard-working, but also rather humorless; they were thrifty but stingy; they prized learning but thought they were a little better than others. All stereotyping aside, however, their impact on Minnesota was crucial. They were mostly low-church Congregationalists, strongly religious but also strongly rationalistic. They valued education, particularly public schools, which in their eyes formed a Protestant bulwark against Catholicism and foreign influence, often seen as the major threats to America.

Yet the Yankee influence was most significant in the area of local government and local leadership. They brought along notions about popular democracy based on a transparent and activist local government. Throughout much of Minnesota, Yankees were among the founding members of most county governments and a majority of city and township governments, especially in southern and western Minnesota. Even in towns where other ethnic groups later predominated and the ever-mobile Yankees moved on to greener pastures, the foundations were often laid by people with roots in old New England.

Yankee political dominance aside, from its origins, Minnesota was a state of great cultural diversity, despite what more recent commentators believe. Before Minnesota became a state, the final draft of the Minnesota Constitution was translated and printed in several languages: German, French, Swedish, Norwegian, Gaelic, and Dakota. (Delegates to the constitutional convention also discussed the possibility of translating the draft into Ojibwe, but this was never realized.)

The opening of Minnesota to European settlement coincided with a surge in immigration from western and northern Europe. Many of the territory's new residents came from these regions.

The largest single group were Germans arriving from a variety of German states. A small but influential group had left Europe following the failed revolutions of 1848. In the mid 1850s, a group of German Freethinkers founded the colony of New Ulm, in the Minnesota River valley. The early colonists centered their social and cultural lives around the *Turnerverein*, or Turner Society, and tried to ban the establishment of any churches within the city limits. Although this effort eventually proved unsuccessful, New Ulm remained a city with a strong Freethinker influence. By contrast, the German settlement around St. Cloud was strongly religious. Although it contained a significant number of German Lutherans and other Protestant faiths, Catholics were in the majority. In 1857 a group of German Benedictine monks and nuns founded what would eventually become a major Minnesota institution, St. John's Abbey. St. John's would grow to be a vital German Catholic center, and the abbey and later university would develop into one of the New World's most significant Benedictine outposts.

Over 12,000 Irish also came to Minnesota by 1860, finding jobs in the infant logging and milling industries as well as taking up farms in various parts of eastern Minnesota. Unlike the Germans or Scandinavians, however, the Irish never formed solid blocs of farming communities, and the greatest number went to cities such as St. Paul.

Minnesota's reputation as a Scandinavian state was yet to be made, but immigrants from Sweden and Norway had already begun to arrive in the Upper Midwest prior to the Civil War. Swedes often found homes and farms in the St. Croix River Valley. Norwegians—some migrating from

Must-See Sites: Marine Mill, Marine-on-St. Croix

Perched on the bluff of the St. Croix River, on a six-acre plot lie remnants of a booming industry long past. In the autumn of 1838 Illinois lumbermen David Hone and Lewis Judd arrived in the St. Croix River valley. Attracted by the area's abundant white pine, they selected this site to build a sawmill and named it after their hometown, Marine, Illinois. Less than one year later on August 24, 1839, the Marine Lumber Company's sawmill cut its first pine log and became the first commercial sawmill in what was to become the state of Minnesota. The sawmill, first run by waterpower and later by steam, operated under many names and owners and milled more than 197 million board feet of lumber by the time it closed in 1895. At that time its frame buildings were torn down and equipment sold to other sawmill companies. Today all that remains are portions of the stone foundations of the once huge sawmill. Interpretive signs, pathways, and an overlook above the ruins provide visitors with a glimpse of the history of this once active industrial site.

Contact: (320) 532-5646; E-mail: marinemill@mnhs.org; Web: www.mnhs.org

Location: Located on Judd Street in the center of Marine-on-St. Croix. Accessible from Minnesota Hwy 95, 11 miles north of Stillwater.

more established communities in Iowa and Wisconsin—filtered into southern and southeastern Minnesota.

Like their German and Irish counterparts, the Scandinavians came, settled, and wrote letters home. These letters would stimulate new waves of immigration. By the time of statehood, 58,728 of Minnesota's 172,023 officially registered residents were foreign-born. In sheer numbers, this was but a trickle. The letters they would write home, however, would soon turn the trickle into a flood.

With settlers beginning to enter the state in larger numbers and the problem of Native American lands apparently solved, Minnesota's leaders set about making a reality of the dream they had sold to the Congress and to themselves. In these years, two men would play a prominent role in the affairs of the new territory. The first was Henry

Sibley, Minnesota's delegate to Congress, and later its first elected governor. He was the archetype of the frontier politician who made a habit of being in the right place at the right time. He made his fortune first through the fur trade and later on commissions from transfers of Native American land. Personable and quick-witted, he was also longer on style than on substance. His style, however, was impressive enough to get himself seated in the U.S. Congress as a delegate from territory that did not yet exist. It was also good enough to get Sibley elected the state's first governor in 1858.

The second was Alexander Ramsey, appointed Minnesota's territorial governor, and later elected its second state governor. A native of Pennsylvania, Ramsey was a young up-and-coming Whig politician. Unlike Sibley, Ramsey was a cool, practical man, more the manager than the bold leader. He emphasized sobriety, good government, and building Minnesota's infrastructure. As U.S. senator and later secretary of war, he was also the state's first politician of national stature. Led by a schemer and speculator in harness with a calm proponent of good government, Minnesota would become a state, and its early course would be marked by both enthusiastic speculation and a desire for a well-run and progressive public life.

In addition to forming a territorial government, Minnesota's political leaders enacted provisions to create a Minnesota Historical Society. This institution would not only archive state documents, but would also have the all important job of recording for posterity the actions of the leaders who had caused it to be formed. Men like Sibley were not, it seems, unaware of the potential of public relations and the ways that myth could take on historical substance.

Of even greater importance, state leaders also created the University of Minnesota in 1851. Although the university would not actually open for another eighteen years, it was the start of one of Minnesota's major institutions. When the state constitution was written it stated that "All the rights, franchises and endowments heretofore granted or conferred on the university of Minnesota are perpetuated onto the university." And so it states to this day, Minnesota having the distinction of being a state with a university and a historical society that predate the state itself.

STATEHOOD

As settlers flooded into newly opened Native American lands, and Minnesota's population swelled, it would only be a matter of time before it reached the threshold necessary for statehood. Its leaders began to draft a constitution. Although based on the U.S. Constitution, the Minnesota Constitution nevertheless reflected some local conditions, such as the issue of whether the state's large Native American population was really part of the state.

The road to full statehood was bumpy. The first major issue would be the boundaries of the state, over which a fierce political battle erupted. Interests in the increasingly populous and Republican southeastern part of Minnesota were not averse to a smaller state, with a northern boundary at the 46th parallel (just north of today's Little Falls). They also sought to move the capital from St. Paul to a site more central to those proposed boundaries: the new town of St. Peter. The bill to move the capital was passed by the legislature, but the official copy of the bill was stolen by Joseph Rollette, a Métis legislator from Pembina in the far north. Rollette hid out and played poker until the legislature adjourned, making the bill effectively void. The U.S. Congress, then controlled by Democrats, fixed the new state's boundaries along the current north–south lines.

On February 26, 1857, the U.S. Congress passed the Minnesota Enabling Act, allowing the citizens to ratify a constitution and elect a state government and be formally admitted.

The Congress' enabling act not only set the state's boundaries, it also provided generous land grants for infrastructure and education improvement—which would become an important factor in the state's economic development. Two sections (240 acres each) of every township were to be used to subsidize public schools (either by using the land for building a school or by selling or renting it and using the proceeds). Land was also allocated to benefit a state university and on which to construct state buildings. Five percent of all public land sales were to be used to build and maintain public roads and other internal improvements. Eventually, land would also be provided to railroads. In some parts of Minnesota, every other section was granted to a private railroad company.

Must-See Sites: Forestville/Mystery Cave State Park, Preston

Visitors to Forestville/Mystery Cave State Park see natural wonders above and below ground. In the summer, beat the heat with a visit below ground where the temperature stays at a constant 48°F. Explore the world of Mystery Cave with its stalactites, stalagmites, and underground pools. Park naturalists provide tours of the cave throughout the summer and on weekends in the spring and fall. Above ground, visitors can see Historic Forestville, a restored 1800s village. Fish three blue-ribbon trout streams for brown trout. Take in the soft pastels of wildflowers in spring or listen to ruffed grouse drumming and wild turkeys gobbling. Hike or bring your horse to ride the ridge tops and stream valleys. Observe interesting geologic features along the way, including sinkholes and the dramatic Big Spring. In the fall, visitors can see the bold colors of the forest. Winter invites visitors to ski or snowmobile the Bluff Country.

Contact: (507) 352-5111; Web: www.dnr.state.mn.us/state_parks/

Location: Approximately 6 miles south of Wykoff. Entrance to the park is 4 miles south of State Highway 16 on Fillmore County Highway 5, then 2 miles east on Fillmore County 118.

With the enabling act in place, the people of Minnesota elected special delegates to write a state constitution. This proved to be a raucous and difficult affair, quite unlike the staid image of good government politics Minnesotans sometimes like to project. Passions between Democrats and the newly formed Republican party were heading to the boiling point nationally over matters such as states' rights and slavery. Locally, both sides wanted to take advantage of the once in a lifetime opportunity provided by the constitution writing process and there was still bad blood over Rollette's trick with the state capital bill.

Eventually, however, the Constitution was written. In October 1857, the overwhelming majority of voters agreed to ratify this founding document. On May 11, 1858, after more political deal making, the U.S. Congress formally admitted Minnesota to the Union.

Left unresolved in the rush to statehood was the status of Minnesota's native inhabitants. The constitution extended the vote to all males age twenty-one and over who were, according to Article VII:

> *First*—Citizens of the United States.
> *Second*—Persons of foreign birth who shall have declared their intention to become citizens.
> *Third*—Persons of mixed white and Indian blood who have adopted the customs and habits of civilization.
> *Fourth*—Persons of Indian blood residing in this state who have adopted the language, customs and habits of civilization, after an examination before any district court in the state, in such manner as shall be provided by law, and shall have been pronounced by said court capable of enjoying the rights of citizenship within the State.

The new state took for its motto the French: *L'Etoile du Nord*—the Star of the North. Given that most of the state had so recently been turned over by the Native Americans, it is little wonder the emblem adopted for the new Minnesota Territory showed an Native American riding off into the sunset while a farmer plows his field. Historian Theodore Blegan quotes a popular poem of the time describing the seal:

> Give way, give way, young warrior,
>   Thou and thy steed give way—
> Rest not, though lingers on the hills
>   The red sun's parting ray.
> The rocky bluff and prairie land
>   The white man claims them now,
> The symbols of his course are here,
>   The rifle, axe, and plough.

These were all reasonable thoughts in 1858, for the state was open to settlement and what was seen as the blessings of civilization, and most of the land that had once been Native American was now in government or private hands. The native peoples were quietly resigned to reservations. The "white man's claim" was a common notion of the time and the poet and most of the state's white residents shared it.

Yet they all would be proven tragically mistaken.

5

Death in the Summer, 1862–65

August on the prairies of western Minnesota is a time of humid, interminable afternoons. Puffy white clouds spot the blue sky and time seems to stand still, broken only by the buzz of cicadas and a westerly breeze. As the sun sinks coloring the western horizon pink, gold, then purple, mosquitoes buzz in people's ears and the shadows grow long. If anything, the nights are more humid, their heat broken only by prairie thunderstorms whose vivid lightning shows roll in the distance long before the rain front arrives.

August of 1862 was no different.

By then, the Civil War had entered its second year and many of the men of Minnesota sent to suppress the Southern rebellion and preserve the Union had seen their share of blood shed. At Bull Run the summer before, the First Minnesota had held the far right of the Union line, and though battered by artillery and musket fire it remained unbroken, one of the few Union regiments able to make that claim after the battle.

Back home, even with the absence of many fathers, husbands, and brothers, life went on. Although settlement in the western part of the state slowed to a trickle, the settlers who were there—a mix of Yankees, and German and Scandinavian immigrants—eked a living out of prairie homesteads. Though these were not comfortable by modern standards, they were more than sufficient for most.

The U.S.–Dakota Tragedy

The settler's Dakota neighbors, however, were starving. Hunting in the summer of 1862 was poor and the gardens the year before had failed. Many Dakota relied on government subsidies, which the Native Americans had accepted in return for their land. The cash payments allowed them to buy food from the local trading posts at Upper and Lower Sioux Agencies. Yet the food was of poor quality and prices were inflated by the merchants and agents to take advantage of the captive market. In addition, the traders pushed cheap liquor, and drinking problems among the Native Americans grew. Since the government payment came only once a year, the Dakota were dependent on credit from these merchants. Year after year, prices went up, and in the merchants' ledger books, the Dakota fell further and further into debt. Each year, increasing amounts of government gold went to the merchants to satisfy these debts, amounts that totaled as much as $80,000 a year.

But in the summer of 1862, the money was late.

Native American families went hungry, eating their dogs and horses, while the agents watched over warehouses full of food. When the promised money did not arrive in June as scheduled, the agents cut off credit to the Dakota.

After the treaty of 1851, the Dakota in Minnesota had moved to their reservation in the Minnesota River valley and lived in peace with a steadily growing number of American settlers. Settler families expected regular friendly visits from their Native American neighbors. Some were so isolated that the Dakota were the only human beings they saw on a regular basis and some even learned to speak the language. Without knowing much English, immigrant settlers had less basis for common communication with the Native Americans and kept more to themselves.

The process of mixing cultures that had begun when the first Frenchman journeyed into the Pays d'en Haut continued. Many Native Americans, encouraged by extra food rations from the Indian agents, cut their hair, built wood or brick houses, and took up farming with horses and plows. Some missionaries and agents treated the Dakota like inferiors. Others, like the Ponds, sought to spread the Gospel but respected and learned from the Dakota, working tirelessly, if not always successfully, to help them adjust to a changing world.

Tribes like the Dakota had never been monolithic. Different bands and leaders always expressed a diversity of opinion. By 1862, these divisions had been furthered by a split between those who tried to hold to the old ways (the so-called Blanket Indians) and a minority who adopted "white ways" (the so-called Farmer Indians). Leaders were often torn as they tried to bridge these differences. One such leader was Taotateduta or Little Crow. His father had signed the infamous treaty of 1805 with which the Americans had secured a legal foothold in Minnesota. His son learned much from the Americans, traveling to New York and Washington and seeing the size and power of American civilization. He was as comfortable in a black suit and hat as in buckskin breeches and moccasins. Like many other Dakota leaders, he knew his people would need to find other ways to survive besides war with the Americans. But he was also ambitious and desired the mantle of leadership and respect of his people.

By 1862, however, leaders like Little Crow had less and less to offer their people, especially their young men. Thanks to the failure of the government subsidies, the leaders and indeed the Dakota as a whole were shown to be powerless. The young people had little to look forward to. Save for occasional clashes with their old enemy the Ojibwe, there were no great adventures, nothing to strive for, and little to hope for. The great traditions of their past, their pride and strength, seemed to count for nothing in this new world.

As the Native Americans grew hungry and some began to fall prey to malnutrition and the sicknesses that went with it, the agents and traders also grew nervous. If the government stopped paying the Dakota, their path to riches would be blocked. The trade was lucrative and many expected to retire to the east in style. So they cut off credit to the Native Americans and closed their warehouses full of food.

The Native American leaders complained to Agent Thomas Galbraith and asked him to give their hungry people food. The agent brushed off their concerns and told them to send their young men hunting and return in a few weeks. In the meantime, Galbraith, sensing the natives' growing anger, went south to Fort Ridgely, a small army outpost just downriver from the Lower Agency. He returned with a company of men from the Fifth Minnesota Infantry. The Dakota hunting parties had had little luck finding food in the already over-hunted prairie. When they returned to the agency, they found it guarded by the soldiers. They managed, however, to persuade the junior officer in command of the troops to open the warehouses. In mid July, the Dakota received just enough food to keep them alive.

As the days passed, the promised money did not appear and many young Dakota men formed a secret Soldiers' Lodge. Disenchanted with the failure of their leaders, they sought refuge in visions of war and violence to avenge the decades of wrongs done to their people and humiliation of watching their hungry parents beg the white traders for food. As the food ran out once again, talk circulated openly of taking the food warehouses by force. On August 4 a large group of armed Dakota confronted the soldiers. Once again, the soldiers intervened with the agents and the traders and convened a meeting between several Dakota chiefs, including Little Crow, Galbraith, and several of the traders. Angry words and veiled threats flew thick and fast. Trader Andrew Myrick, asked to give some of his stores to the hungry Dakota, retorted, "If they are hungry, let them eat grass or their own dung."

Finally, the warehouses were opened again, providing just enough food to keep the Dakota from dying. The tension eased and the troops returned to Fort Ridgely. On August 17, unbeknownst to the Dakota, the traders, or the agents, a government supply wagon with $71,000 in gold began its slow journey from St. Paul to the reservation.

It would not be in time.

That same day, four young Dakota went out hunting. They had little luck, but one of them came across a settler's clutch of chicken eggs. An argument ensued over whether to take the eggs. One young man said it wrong to take them and that the settlers would be upset. The others taunted him and called him a coward. He responded by insisting that he was not a coward and would prove it by killing a white man. More bluster ensued and the four eventually came on a local postmaster and store owner, Robinson Jones. They challenged Jones to a friendly round of target shooting. Jones agreed. In the middle of the contest, Jones fired at the target and when he did not immediately reload, the four Dakota turned on him and shot him dead. They shot a neighbor and Jones' wife and then fled, leaving two other terrified women behind.

TAOYATEDUTA IS NOT A COWARD

When the four returned to the reservation and told their story, it started an uproar. Soldiers would surely come to find the killers. They might hold all Dakota responsible and the government might withhold their money. Yet killing the whites had been easy and most of the army was away fighting the war. Long acrimonious debates ensued most of the night. Several older chiefs counseled against further action, knowing that the Dakota courted disaster. But the actions of the young men excited many people weary of humiliation and broken promises. The young men of the Soldiers' Lodge were for war. Finally, they took the matter to Little Crow. Although no chief could, by himself, decide for war or peace, Little Crow retained greater prestige than many of his fellow chiefs. He had proven an able spokesman and knew both white and Native American ways.

The war party spoke in favor of killing all the whites, driving the settlers from the valley, and inviting other tribes to join them. In the darkness of the summer night, they spun visions of a people that could again be great. But those who spoke for peace poured scorn on the idea, pointing out that it was folly, suicide. With the Soldiers' Lodge howling for war and the older chiefs counseling moderation, Little Crow spoke, calling the war party fools and children. One of the war party called him a coward. His answer, as reported by those who remembered it, began with a dark prophecy:

> Taoyateduta is not a coward and he is not a fool…. You are full of the white man's devil-water. You are like dogs in the Hot Moon when they run mad and snap at their own shadows. We are only little herds of buffalo left scattered; the great herds that once covered the prairies are no more. See!—the white men are like locusts when they fly so thick that the whole sky is a snowstorm…. Kill one—two—ten, and ten times ten will come to kill you…. You are fools…. You will die like rabbits when the hungry wolves hunt them in the Hard Moon.

The peace faction was elated at his powerful rhetoric, which seemed enough to sway the debate. But Little Crow was not finished, and why he spoke the next words no one can ever be completely sure. "Taoyateduta is not a coward," he said again. "He will die with you."

Little Crow, 1860

When Little Crow sided with the war faction it split the Dakota, isolated the peace faction, and cast the die for war. Those who did not support the war, who were especially strong at the Upper Agency, now withdrew, leaving the "hawks" to pursue their plans. Little Crow, as the most forceful of the Dakota chiefs, may have been swayed by a sense of duty to lead his people into war he knew they would lose. He may have felt he could control the dogs of war once they had been let slip. He was surely influenced by the years of mistreatment and humiliation inflicted on the Dakota. Yet Little Crow also craved popularity and the status of being a chief, and he may have feared a loss of status with the youngest and most energetic of his young men more than the potential disaster their actions courted. It was this weakness that caused him to side with the warriors.

The survivors of the day's attack had managed to go for help at Fort Ridgely, but few believed that the peaceful Dakota would do such a thing. At worst it was the action of a few drunken braves who would soon be brought to justice. Many settlers got advance warning of what was to come from Dakota friends or neighbors. Some heeded the warning, while others did not. Even for those who prepared to leave for safer locations, by the morning of August 18 it was often already too late.

Shortly after 6 AM a large group of armed Dakota men appeared at the Lower Agency. Without warning the Dakota attacked the small community of white and mixed-race merchants, artisans, and their families. Among the first to fall was trader Andrew Myrick.

His body was found with its mouth stuffed full of grass.

The helpless traders were caught completely by surprise without time to resist. Only a handful escaped death, either due to luck or to Dakota friends who saved their lives. A French ferryman who risked his life to get several families across the Minnesota River was later found beheaded and mutilated. A large group of Dakota men and women pillaged the stores at Lower Sioux and then set the buildings on fire.

Groups of angry and often drunken Dakota warriors spread out in all directions, attacking isolated cabins. They killed men, women, children, even infants, and in one case an unborn child. The victims were shot, beheaded, axed, disemboweled, and burned or flayed alive. Groups of settlers ranging from thirty or forty to a few individuals were set upon and killed. But there was no pattern. In some instances, the women and children were taken prisoner. Some women were raped repeatedly, others unharmed. A few individuals who spoke Dakota were able to successfully plead for their lives. Some settlers showed shameful cowardice. One man fled when the Dakota attacked his family. As he fled he ordered his fifteen-year-old son to stay behind and fight while he rode the only horse to safety.

Tremendous heroes also emerged, including many Dakota who risked their lives to save their fellow human beings. John Other Day was known as one of the most redoubtable Dakota warriors, and also as an advocate for peace. He protected the whites at Upper Sioux Agency. His tough reputation kept other Dakota at bay and he later spirited 62 people away from danger. Chief Chaska hid Sarah Wakefield in his own home, saving her life several times.

German immigrant Justina Krieger saw her husband and neighbors killed and watched as Dakota tore her niece apart while the child was still alive. She was shot in the back and survived an attempted disemboweling. With virtually no food, water, or assistance, Krieger crawled and stumbled for miles across the prairie past scores of mutilated corpses. Other women and children, taken captive by the Dakota, survived from day to day.

As the first frightened refugees reached Fort Ridgely, a group of forty-six soldiers was dispatched to suppress what was still believed to be an isolated incident. The commanding officer, Captain John Marsh, refused to believe the tales of many of the refugees and marched straight to the Lower Agency. After all, the Dakota were mere "savages" who could never stand up to regular soldiers. At the Minnesota River crossing, Marsh's men walked into a well-planned ambush. Scores of soldiers fell right away and the rest of the command fled south in disarray, pursued by the Dakota. Marsh died trying to get back across the river, and only a handful of his command made it back to the fort.

Little Crow and the other Dakota leaders realized that their only hope of success was to dislodge the Americans from their posts at Fort Ridgely and New Ulm. Yet many Dakota fighters, especially those led by the most militant chiefs, were spread out across the prairie, attacking isolated homesteads as far away as Lake Shetek, Sioux Falls, and Hutchinson. Nor did other Sioux bands living to the west seem interested in joining the uprising, although a few volunteers did arrive. Other tribes such as the Ho-Chunk and Ojibwe were even less interested in joining the war effort. Yet the Dakota leaders knew that they had to strike the outposts quickly and clear the Minnesota River valley before their enemies could regroup.

Meanwhile, as news of the uprising spread eastward to New Ulm, St. Peter, and St. Paul, confusion reigned. Thousands of terrified and injured refugees flooded in. A company of haphazardly armed militia was organized at St. Peter and, led by a local judge, Charles Flandrau, set out for New Ulm. In St. Paul, once the scope of the disaster became clear and the news of the destruction of Marsh's command received, Governor Ramsey placed former territorial governor Henry Sibley in command of Minnesota forces.

Sibley faced many problems. He had few troops, poorly trained, with minimal supplies. He faced these obstacles with all the energy of a midwestern George McClellan. Sibley sent a regular stream of letters complaining about the lack of supplies and promising to advance toward the threatened area. Days passed as panic spread throughout the state and Sibley did nothing.

Meanwhile, the Dakota, with several hundred warriors under Chiefs Little Crow and Mankato planned to attack Ridgely and New Ulm. Both locations were defended only by scratch forces of soldiers and armed settlers. Despite its name, Fort Ridgely was merely a collection of buildings without a stockade, while New Ulm was a small, new town in a position that was difficult to defend.

The first blow fell at New Ulm on August 19 when about 150 Dakota attacked the poorly armed garrison of German settlers. Despite being outnumbered and heavily pressed, the immigrants held their ground, thanks in large part to the multiple leaders that led the Native American attacks. Divided in their opinions, the Dakota leaders were unable to launch a coordinated all-out assault on the town. That evening, the St. Peter militia under Judge Flandrau reached New Ulm.

The following morning, Little Crow managed to gather a force of about 400 Dakota to launch a concerted attack on Fort Ridgely, which was defended by about 180 soldiers and militia and sheltered almost 300 refugees. During the previous day, the fort's defenders had managed to build a few barricades, but their main defensive weapons were six cannon, including a big twenty-four pounder.

The Dakota advanced close to the exposed fort through nearby ravines and attacked. A classic military firing line of soldiers scattered for cover under the Native Americans' withering fire. The first attack was driven back by the soldiers, aided by the cannon, which had a demoralizing effect on the Dakota. A second attack was also driven back, although the Dakota managed to set fire to a few outlying buildings. During the fighting there was no quarter asked or given. Historian Duane Schultz relates:

> At dusk, several Indians entered the old stables.... J. C. Whipple fired two shells at the stables, both of which exploded inside, setting the hay on fire. Joe Latour and George Dashner, two mixed bloods who had stayed to defend the fort, saw the fire from [a] bakery nearby. An Indian ran out of the stables' door, heading for the ravine. Dashner took aim and hit him. He fell to the ground and started to crawl away. Dashner and Latour ran to him, picked him up by the arms and legs, and threw him headlong into the flames.

Native Americans rarely fought as they are shown in Hollywood movies. Their form of war emphasized stealth—and quickness. Man for man, the Dakota were as good if not better than the soldiers and militia. They knew the countryside and used the terrain to advance under cover and never made reckless charges. However, against a fortified, alert foe they had few options. As the long history of Native American wars demonstrated, they could often win impressive victories over American soldiers, but could not sustain long wars.

Little Crow and the other Dakota leaders realized this and knew they needed to take the Minnesota River valley quickly. On August 22, an even larger force of Dakota, perhaps 800, attacked Fort Ridgely. A series of concerted attacks pressed the defenders to their limit, but each time

Must-See Sites: W.W. Mayo House, Le Sueur

The stories of Mayo Clinic and the Green Giant Company began in this modest home in Le Sueur. Costumed guides explain the history of the home and tell the stories of the Mayo and Cosgrove families who lived there before founding the Mayo Clinic and Green Giant. W. W. Mayo hand-built the Gothic-style house in 1859 and set up his first medical practice in an upstairs room. In 1863 Dr. Mayo was appointed examining surgeon for the Minnesota Civil War draft board, headquartered in Rochester. Later, Dr. Mayo and his sons founded the Mayo Clinic in Rochester. In 1874 the Cosgroves moved into the home. In 1903 Carson Nesbit Cosgrove conducted the organizational meeting and later served as the head of the Minnesota Valley Canning Company, which became the Green Giant Company in 1950.

Contact: Phone: (507) 665-3250 or -6965; E-mail: mayohouse@mnhs.org; Web: www.mnhs.org

Location: 118 N. Main Street, Le Sueur.

the Dakota attacks were broken up by deadly canister shot from the cannons. Three defenders were killed in the assault and thirteen wounded. Dakota losses are unknown.

Chief Big Eagle was later quoted as saying "We thought the fort was the door to the valley as far as St. Paul, and if we got through the door nothing could stop us this side of the Mississippi. But the defenders of the fort were very brave and kept the door shut." With the repulse at the fort, the Dakota stood little chance of victory.

Yet the danger had not fully passed. Sibley had managed to get his command as far as St. Peter and then halted—despite urgent pleas for help from New Ulm—to send more letters off to St. Paul, demanding more supplies and more troops. On August 23, the Dakota attempted to seize New Ulm once again. The garrison, now under the command of Flandrau and consisting entirely of poorly armed militia, some carrying only pitchforks, had spent the previous few days drilling and building makeshift fortifications. Still, some of the 300-odd militiamen were as much a danger to themselves as to an attacker, and they had no idea if the Dakota had taken Fort Ridgely, whence they had heard the sounds of fierce fighting the day before.

The Dakota attacked throughout the day, and the defenders began to suffer serious losses. One by one, New Ulm's buildings went up in flames. Fighting became house-to-house. At about 4:30 the Dakota seized a strongly built log house and smithy that would allow them to finally break the defensive perimeter. A group of sixty men launched a desperate counterattack. Jacob Nix, one of those who made the charge, wrote in his German-language account:

> Here ensued a terrible and bloody struggle which meant life or death. Here in just a few minutes, the fate of the town was in the balance. The Indians, even though they outnumbered us four to one, were driven out of the blockhouse and several other nearby buildings.

The charge broke the Native American position, forcing them to fall back. As darkness fell, the defenders set fire to the remaining buildings outside of their defensive perimeter, casting an eerie light over the scene. The defenders had lost 32 dead and over 60 wounded. The Dakota slipped away in the night.

SIBLEY'S "OFFENSIVE"

On August 25, New Ulm's 1,500 defenders and the refugees abandoned the city for fear of further attacks and fell back to St. Peter in a procession of wagon, buggies, and carts, carrying the wounded with them. By this time, Sibley had collected a force of over 1,300 men, including 400 cavalry. Finally, on August 27, after being excoriated by press and politicians, Sibley marched his command south and reached Fort Ridgely the following day. By this time, panic had given way to rage and calls for revenge, even genocide. Virtually every newspaper in the state joined in the chorus. Jane Grey Swisshelm, the editor of the *St. Cloud Democrat*, a noted feminist and crusader for the rights of enslaved African Americans, was not alone in calling for the extermination of Minnesota's Native Americans.

The Dakota under Little Crow had fallen back to the vicinity north of the Upper Agency, not only warriors but women, children, old people, and some 250 white and mixed-race hostages. There, a virtual civil war was brewing. Following the reverses at Fort Ridgely and New Ulm, those Dakota who had opposed the war tried to keep some of Little Crow's followers from killing the hostages and from involving the entire Dakota nation in further disaster. On more than one occasion, the conflict almost resulted in bloodshed.

As the Dakota argued among themselves, Sibley sat at Fort Ridgely. Whether he continued to overestimate the size of the enemy, felt his troops needed more training, or sought a negotiated release of the captives is not clear. However, after several days of quiet, Sibley was confident enough to send a burial detachment of 160 men to the Lower Agency. It was a costly blunder. Near a small stream called Birch Cooley, close to the site of the present-day town of Morton, the detachment was ambushed by a large force of Dakota. Cut off, with limited ammunition and water, the soldiers made barricades of the bodies of their own horses. Only the sound of gunfire, echoing back down the valley, alerted the troops at Fort Ridgely, who sent out a relief force. By the time it arrived the next morning, 22 more soldiers were dead and the burial party was down to its last rounds of ammunition. The Dakota slipped away again, suffering only light losses. In the meantime, the Dakota routed another small party of soldiers near the town of Forest City. To the north, Native Americans attacked Fort Abercrombie and in the south burned the abandoned town of Sioux Falls.

With the nation in the midst of a civil war, the federal government could spare little help for Minnesota, but did manage to send General John Pope to take command. Pope had failed against the Confederates at Second Bull Run and his presence added little to the state's defense. More significant was the arrival of a battle-tested Minnesota regiment, the Third Minnesota, pulled from the front lines in Tennessee to quell the uprising back home.

On September 19, Sibley, now in command of over 1,600 men, set out from Fort Ridgely. Again he advanced slowly and with extreme caution, pausing each evening to dig rifle pits around his camp. As Sibley's army moved closer to the Upper Agency, Little Crow managed to pull together several hundred Dakota who wanted to continue the fight. On September 23, as the army approached, the Native Americans laid an ambush for the army near Wood Lake. A forging party from the Third Minnesota, looking to supplement their rations, stumbled across the ambush and raised the alarm. For the next few hours a confused clash took place between Native Americans and soldiers. Several soldiers were killed and 34 wounded. On the other side, Mankato, one of the Dakota's most able leaders, lost his life.

With no chance to defeat a much larger army, the war faction among the Dakota fell apart and Little Crow and his followers broke into small bands and fled west. Sibley regrouped his men and eventually managed to cover the distance to a location near today's town of Montevideo and free the captives three days later.

Perhaps several hundred people had died in the massacres, many killed in the most horrible ways imaginable. The exact numbers will never be known, as no accurate count of the scattered population had been made prior to the massacres and afterward many bodies were never recovered—either lost or consumed by prairie fires or wild animals. Some eyewitnesses the following summer reported heaps of human bones bleached in the sun. Some 40,000 people had fled the western and central sections of the state. Yet the tragedy was not over.

Although some of those who had committed atrocities were killed, captured, or surrendered, the majority of Native Americans remaining in the reservation had played little part in the war. In fact many had opposed it. Despite the pleas of some of the newly released captives, there was little effort to distinguish the guilty from the innocent, the bystanders from the perpetrators. A military court sentenced 307 Native Americans to death. Most of the trials barely lasted a few minutes and the evidence against many was virtually non-existent. It was enough that they were Native Americans. In November, all the remaining Dakota from the reservation, nearly 1,700 mostly old men, women, and children, were rounded up and marched east to Fort Snelling. At the town of Henderson, the Dakota were set upon by a mob. Duane Schultz writes:

Famous Minnesotans: Sinclair Lewis

Born Feb. 7, 1885, Sauk Centre, Minn.
Died Jan. 10, 1951, Rome, Italy.

Sinclair Lewis was one of Minnesota's most famous literary sons, but paradoxically he is most noted for books that sneered at the lifestyle of a majority of the state's residents. Born in Sauk Centre to a local doctor, Lewis was educated locally and worked for the city's newspapers before leaving to attend Oberlin College and later Yale. He wrote for a variety of publications, held a range of odd jobs, and even spent time at Upton Sinclair's utopian socialist commune. Beginning in 1914, he published a series of five novels, none of which garnered much attention. In 1920, he published *Main Street*, his best-known novel and described by some as an attempt to write an American version of *Madame Bovary*. Set in a fictional town, Gopher Prairie, the book was really about Sauk Centre as remembered by the youthful Lewis. It portrayed the town and its people as dull and narrow-minded nobodies who quashed all creativity in themselves and others. In reality, Lewis had grasped only a portion of small-town life, and his portrait evinces an incomplete understanding of Sauk Centre. Nevertheless, the work was highly popular with those who saw the countryside as a place of intellectual darkness and it helped to shape popular opinion of small-town life. Lewis went on to publish other novels in a similar vein: *Babbitt*, which attacked middle-class business men; *Arrowsmith*, which took on commercialized science; and *Elmer Gantry* which lambasted evangelical Protestantism. His later novels—eleven after *Elmer Gantry*—were not nearly as successful. In 1930 he became the first American awarded the Nobel Prize in Literature. Despite his portrayal of the town, Lewis returned to Sauk Centre and Minnesota frequently, and the town now, perversely, promotes itself as the original *Main Street*. After Lewis' death his ashes were buried in Sauk Centre.

Sam Brown recalled that the streets were "crowded with and angry and excited populace, cursing, shouting, and crying. Men, women, and children armed with guns, knives, clubs, and stones rushed upon the Indians as the [wagon] train was passing by, and before the soldiers could interfere and stop them, succeeded in pulling many of the old men and women and even children from the wagons and by the hair of the head and beating them.... I saw an enraged white woman rush up to one of the wagons and snatch a nursing babe from its mother's breast and dash it violently against the ground."

The soldiers dragged the white woman away and handed the battered infant back to it mother; it died within a few hours. A drunken white man approached a wagon and aimed his pistol at Sam Brown's uncle, at one of the friendly Indians who has helped save the white captives. Colonel Marshall rode up, his saber drawn, and knocked the man's gun out of his hand.

At Fort Snelling, the captives were confined to a small area, muddy and cold. Disease broke out and quickly spread among the Dakota, claiming many lives. Meanwhile, the condemned prisoners were marched to Mankato, barely surviving their own brushes with lynch mobs.

In Washington, Bishop Henry Whipple made a direct appeal to President Abraham Lincoln to spare the lives of the condemned Native Americans. Lincoln agreed to review the cases and proceeded to commute the sentences of all but 38 of the men. On December 26, in the largest mass execution in American history, the 38 Native Americans were hung on a specially constructed gallows. Among those killed was Chief Chaska, who had opposed the war and who had saved the life of settler Sarah Wakefield.

Minnesota troops continued to scour the western part of the state for any Native Americans. On September 16, 1863, the commander of the Minnesota Mounted Rangers, Colonel Samuel McPhail, ordered one of his subordinates:

You will march tomorrow... to Kandegohi [Kandyohi] Lakes with your command and detect if possible the presence of any hostile Indians in the vicinity, and should you meet such Indians you will fall upon them and destroy them, and should Indians having fired upon your command in any event surrender as prisoners, you

will hang them by the neck to the first tree until dead.
Leave their bodies hanging and report the fact to these
Head Quarters.

State troops would continue to mount expeditions in the
Dakotas as late as 1866. Little Crow, now a broken old
man, escaped to the Dakotas and then to Canada. In the
summer of 1863 he and a few followers slipped back into
Minnesota. While he and his son were picking berries they
were ambushed by two white settlers and the chief was
shot and killed. His body was later identified, scalped, and
publicly displayed.

The Dakota prisoners at Fort Snelling were later
shipped to Nebraska, to a miserable patch of land where
many more died from sickness and hunger. Nor were they
alone. In 1864 the Ho-Chunk people of southern Minnesota
were also deported to Nebraska, even though they had
never participated in the war. In the north, only the Ojibwe
remained of the state's native inhabitants. For the first time
in perhaps seven centuries, there were almost no Dakota in
Minnesota and many believed they would never again live
in the state.

THE FIRST MINNESOTA

As the tragedies mounted in the state, the Civil War began to
overshadow all else. Many of Minnesota's young men were in
the east and the south, shedding blood to preserve the Union.
Among the first to answer President Lincoln's call for
volunteers were the men of the First Minnesota, who would
for serve three years. Pioneer farmers from frontier counties,
shopkeepers from St. Paul and Stillwater, German and
Swedish immigrants, Yankees and Irish, they marched east in
May 1861. Joining the Army of the Potomac, they saw action
at First Bull Run, the Peninsular Campaign, and bloody
Antietam, becoming hardened veterans.

In the summer of 1863, the First Minnesota, smaller in
numbers due to disease and battles, marched north into
Pennsylvania along with the rest of the Army of the
Potomac. Behind them came Robert E. Lee and the
victorious Army of Northern Virginia. By invading the
North, Lee sought to deliver a knock-out to Union hopes of
a military victory. Union forces under Gen. George Meade

desperately searched for favorable ground to halt Lee's advance. On July 1, 1863, the advance forces of both armies met at Gettysburg.

Minnesota soldier James Wright remembered the Union army as "way-worn and foot-sore for nearly a month of marching; weather-beaten, soil-stained, dirty and ragged from tramping and camping in heat and in dust, in rain and in mud, by day and by night." This time, however, the Union forces had reached the field in time, and throughout the day of June 1 both tested their opponents.

The morning of July 2 found the First Minnesota, along with the rest of the Union Second Corps, under the command of Gen. Winfield Scott Hancock, holding the center of the Union line on Cemetery Ridge. With a few companies detached for picket duty, the regiment mustered a mere 262 men. This small regiment, commanded by Col. William Colville, was put in the reserve of the Union position and held there throughout the morning and afternoon of the fatal day.

Wright recalled the scene: "Crashing, crushing, stunning discharges of artillery made the earth vibrate beneath us. Rolling, tearing, crackling volleys of musketry—Union cheers and Confederate yells, mingling with other noises of the strife—burst out from the concealing clouds of smoke." The Minnesotans watched and waited as the battle raged.

The sun began its slow descent into the west, where far away from Gettysburg the wives, parents, and children of the First Minnesota were finishing their day's work and preparing for dinner. Already the day had seen some of the fiercest fighting in American history. Union forces had repelled Rebel attacks on Little Round Top in desperate hand-to-hand fighting. In front of the Minnesota position, the Devil's Den, the Wheat Field, and the Peach Orchard were scenes of slaughter as fighting raged back and forth.

Finally, an hour before sunset, a last Rebel attack, led by A. P. Hill's Corps, broke through the Union position in the center, tearing a gaping hole in the line. Hill sent two brigades into this gap. When his Alabamans and Floridians reached the top of Cemetery Ridge, the Union position— and the battle—would be lost.

Gen. Hancock saw Hill's men coming and knew that

Union reinforcements rushing to the scene would never make it in time to plug the hole. Then Hancock saw a small force of 262 men in blue at the top of the ridge.

"My God!" Hancock said, riding up, "Are these all the men we have here? What regiment is this?"

"The First Minnesota," replied Col. Colville.

"Colonel, do you see those colors?" Hancock asked, pointing to the advancing Alabama battle flags. Colville replied that he could. "Then advance colonel, and take those colors!"

Bayonets fixed, the First moved forward in line, double quick, toward the mass of Rebel attackers. Shots and shells tore holes in the Minnesota line. "Bullets whistled past us," remembered a veteran, "shells screech over us... comrade after comrade dropped from the ranks; but on the line went." Isaac Taylor from Belle Prairie was cut down by a Confederate shell just feet away from his brother Henry, who would bury him two days later.

Closing on the Rebel line, the Minnesotans charged into the heart of an Alabama brigade 1,600 strong. Seeing a force appear out of the smoke, advancing silently with bayonets fixed, threw the Confederate front ranks into confusion and their advance halted. Colville ordered his men to fire, point blank, into the gray line.

The Alabamans staggered but came on again, and the Minnesotans took cover and began a steady fire. In moments, the outnumbered First was encircled, consumed by a storm of fire. Colville fell and his second in command took charge for only a moment before he, too, was shot down.

Five minutes passed and still the First held its ground. Officers, color bearers, and privates fell one after another. Ten minutes passed.

The Confederate brigade commander, seeing his attack halted, unsure of Union strength, and lacking flank support, ordered his men to fall back and regroup.

Seeing the Rebel pressure weaken, the wounded Colville ordered his only remaining officer to pull back to the ridge. By then Union reinforcements were arriving on the scene to close the gap in the line. The Minnesotans fell back, still carrying their colors. At the top of Cemetery Ridge, out of 262 men, only 47 remained standing. In less than 15 minutes, 82 percent of the First Minnesota's men were killed or wounded, but they had saved the Union from disaster. Perhaps never in U.S. military history did any other unit face such odds and suffer such casualties.

Later, Gen. Hancock stated:

> I had no alternative but to order the regiment in…. I saw that in some way five minutes must be gained…. It was fortunate that I found so grand a body of men as the First Minnesota. I knew they must lose heavily and it caused me pain to give the order for them to advance, but I would have done if I had known every man would be killed. It was a sacrifice that must be made. The superb gallantry of those men saved our line from being broken. No soldiers, on any field, in this or any other country, ever displayed grander heroism.

Throughout the war, Minnesota sent some 25,000 men to support the Union, or one tenth of its 250,000 residents (in 1865), including eleven infantry regiments along with special formations of artillery, cavalry, and sharpshooters. Although the First Minnesota served in the east and perhaps earned the greatest fame, most Minnesota troops served in the western campaigns. At the Battle of Corinth in October 1862, the Fifth Minnesota saved the Union's right flank from being defeated. The single largest concentration of Minnesota troops gathered in combat at the battle of Nashville in December 1864 when the Fifth, Seventh, Ninth, and Tenth fought nearly shoulder to shoulder in the last major battle in the West.

Despite all the glory lavished on the troops by historians, for most men, the war was a hardship and death came more commonly from disease than bullets. During the siege of Vicksburg, for example, the Fourth Minnesota was reduced to half strength due to sickness. The Sixth Minnesota suffered no battlefield casualties, but lost 121 men to malaria in southern Illinois in the summer of 1864.

The war also had an often overlooked impact on many of the state's young men: They had the formative experiences of their life away from home and family. But there they formed close bonds with comrades. This feeling of comradeship was indeed a major reason many veterans re-enlisted after their tours of duty were finished. Edward Bassett of the First Minnesota was mustered out in February 1864 with the rest of his hard-fighting regiment.

On the farm in southern Minnesota, he wrote: "Home again, home again. I slept in my old bed last night, and feel some better this morn. It looks dreary outdoors. I wish the trees were growing and the flowers in bloom. I almost wish I was back in the old camp for a few hours." A year later Bassett re-enlisted in the First Minnesota Heavy Artillery.

In the years to come, these men, joined by many other Civil War veterans from other states, would form a crucial element of the leadership of the state.

By 1865, Minnesota's deadly summers finally came to an end. They brought the state and its people tragedy and bloodshed that many wished to forget, but which others sought to mythologize. Although the Civil War had been fought for noble reasons and the ancestors of Dred Scott, one of Minnesota's first African Americans, were free from slavery, the U.S.–Dakota War had no such conclusions. There were no winners and no righteous causes to relieve the darkness and tragedy. Although the Dakota people would in time return to the state (a remarkable story that has yet fully to be told), the war marked the end of a way of life that had persevered in Minnesota for centuries.

Must-See Sites: Birch Cooley Battlefield/Lower Sioux Agency, Morton

On Sept. 2, 1862, a peaceful field in southern Minnesota near the town of Morton was the scene of a fierce battle between the U.S. Army and Dakota warriors. The Dakota kept U.S. soldiers under siege for 36 hours before a relief detachment arrived from Fort Ridgely. The site offers a self-guided trail through recreated prairie where visitors can read about the battle from the perspectives of Joseph Anderson, a captain in the U.S. Army, and Wamditanka (Big Eagle), a Mdewakanton soldier. Sketches from soldier Albert Colgrave provide vivid battle details. Guideposts help pinpoint where the U.S. soldiers were camped and the positions the Dakota took to surround the U.S. soldiers. Learn more about the U.S.–Dakota War at the nearby Fort Ridgely Historic Site and about the history of the Dakota people and the causes of the war at the Lower Sioux Agency Historic Site.

Contact: (507) 697-6321; E-mail: birchcoulee@mnhs.org; Web: www.mnhs.org

Location: Three miles north of Morton, at the junction of Renville County Hwys 2 and 18, one mile east of U.S. Highway 71.

6

GOD'S COUNTRY

In the years after the Civil War and the Dakota War, Minnesotans tried to put the horrors of war and massacre behind them. The rest of the state's history was far more staid, save for an occasional episode such as when Jesse James and his gang tried to rob a bank in Northfield in 1876 and were decimated by a swarm of armed citizens. The result of all the bloodshed of the early 1860s was a "solving" of the "Indian problem," and there was little sympathy for those who seemed to stand in the way of the nation's progress. Yet the greatest changes in Minnesota were still to come.

In the half century following statehood, migrants and immigrants flooded into the state, transforming Minnesota completely. Much of what had been before now disappeared or was altered almost beyond recognition, often within the space of a few years. The prairie ecosystem, which had dominated much of Minnesota's landscape for millennia, vanished save for a few small pockets. Large areas of the northern forests were cut to feed America's demand for wood, and great seams of iron ore were opened. Duluth changed from a sleepy village to a major inland port, while St. Paul and Minneapolis became the miller, hog butcher, and rail hub of the region, if not the nation.

In the 1860s, the population of the state more than doubled, reaching nearly half a million by 1870. Despite a decade of grasshopper plagues, by 1880 Minnesota had nearly 800,000 inhabitants. In 1890 the state's population stood at 1.3 million and by 1900 it reached 1.7 million. Minnesota's urban population grew even more dramatically. Between 1870 and 1880, the populations of St. Paul and Stillwater each more than doubled. Minneapolis's population expanded 3.5 times, from 13,000 in 1870 to nearly 47,000 in 1880.

Wheat, Wood, and Iron

The first fuel for this expansion was wheat. Although today most of the state's cropland is devoted to soybeans, corn, or sugarbeets, in the late nineteenth century, wheat was king. By 1870 Minnesota was the third largest spring wheat producing state in America, with much of its production occurring in a triangle whose apex was St. Paul, stretching south through Mankato and Winona to the Iowa border. By 1879, 3 million acres were sown with spring or winter wheat. The state's crop grew from 2 million bushels in 1860 to 18.6 million in 1870 and then to 52.3 million in 1890. Wheat shipments by rail and river from Winona alone grew eight-fold between 1860 and 1866.

Historian Theodore Blegen recorded one visitor to Hastings as claiming there was "wheat everywhere.... wagon loads of wheat pouring down to the levee; wheat in the streets; wheat on the sidewalks." And one minister wrote: "Cottage Grove has gone to wheat. Men work in wheat all day when it does not rain, lounge about talking about wheat when it is wet, dream about wheat at night and I fear go to meeting Sabbath Day to think about wheat." From southeast Minnesota, the kingdom of wheat expanded west to the Dakota border and north to the Red River valley.

Just as many new Minnesotans were drawn to the farmer's frontier on the prairies, others were drawn north to work the timber and mining frontier. The settlement of farm land was the story of common men and women with dreams of a better life for their families. The state's extractive industries were built on the plans of a few entrepreneurs and a great deal of capital investment.

Although logging began to draw both loggers and investors to Minnesota when it was still a territory, the heyday of lumbering in the state occurred in the decades after the Civil War. The stands of hardwood in the central and eastern parts of the state, interspersed with bits of open grassland, were attractive to settlers who could not only use the local timber for homes, fences, and fuel, but could sell off the excess wood to earn income in the early years of the homestead. The land underneath was fertile enough to grow good crops. The further north one went, however, the worse the soil and the greater the timber. Early loggers and pioneers found vast stands of white pine, a wood that would build the towns and cities of the Upper Midwest. Daniel Stanchfield, a native of Maine and one of the first to survey the northern forests with an eye toward logging stated, "Seventy mills in seventy years couldn't exhaust the white pine I have seen on the Rum River."

Investors from New England and immigrant entrepreneurs like the German Frederick Weyerhauser set up scores of saw mills across the state, but especially at key river and rail junctions such as Stillwater, Winona, and, most importantly, Minneapolis. Gangs of men went north to cut the pine and to work in the mills. Some made a career of it. For others, particularly farmers seeking to supplement their income during the winter months, it was a temporary stint.

The state's lumber production skyrocketed. By 1876 Minnesota produced 193 million board feet. Historian Agnes Larson calculated that this was enough lumber to circle the earth one and half times with one-foot wide boards. But this was just the beginning. When the state's lumber production peaked in 1905, Minnesota produced 2 billion board feet. The wood of these trees not only brought state businessmen great wealth, but it quite literally built the towns and cities of the Midwest and of America.

While the value or potential value of Minnesota's timber and farming were known or imagined before statehood, the state's third great extractive industry was a relative latecomer. The idea of rich ore deposits around Lake Superior was theorized early on, and Native Americans had for centuries worked naturally occurring pieces of copper into jewelry and other useful and beautiful objects. Early European and American explorers imagined mines of gold, silver, and copper. Although huge copper deposits were found in Michigan's Upper Peninsula, and silver and gold attracted much attention, no significant deposits were ever found in Minnesota.

Many early prospectors who surveyed the state for mineral wealth saw that northern Minnesota geology was right for iron ore but walked right over some of North America's largest deposits of iron ore without knowing it. Most geologists and miners simply assumed that iron ore would be underground and brought to the surface in traditional shaft mines. Much of Minnesota's iron ore,

Must-See Sites: Oliver Kelly Farm, Elk River

Step onto a working 1860s farm, pick heirloom vegetables from the garden, visit the farmhands and animals at the barn, or churn butter and see what's cooking in the farmhouse. Costumed guides work the fields with oxen and horses. At different times throughout the season, visitors can see plowing with oxen, horse-powered threshing, haymaking, and other harvest activities. The gardens and fields are filled with many of the same plants the Kelley farm grew over 130 years ago. Animals similar to those raised by pioneer families fill the barn and outbuildings. In the house, visitors can try domestic crafts like making straw hats and soap.

Contact: (763) 441-6896; E-mail: kelleyfarm@mnhs.org; Web: www.mnhs.org

Location: 2.5 miles southeast of downtown Elk River on U.S. Hwy 10.

however, was on the surface, almost unimaginably easy to merely scoop up and process. It was not until the 1860s and 1870s, however, that mineralogists and business people started to wake up to the possibilities. The Vermillion Range was discovered in the 1860s (though its full extent was not yet clear) and the Mesabi Range in the 1870s. The Cuyuna Range, with more traditional deep seams of ore and rich in manganese, was not definitively located until the 1890s.

The opening of Lake Superior shipping to the rest of the Great Lakes and the development of the ports of Duluth and Superior, Wisconsin, as well as rail transport from the mines to the ports, made Minnesota's Iron Range possible. To develop this infrastructure, however, required a great influx of eastern capital and men like Charlemange Tower (for whom the town of Tower was named), Jay Cooke, J. Pierpont Morgan, Andrew Carnegie, James J. Hill, and John D. Rockefeller were among those who invested in Minnesota mining. Companies like U.S. Steel, Federal Steel, Minnesota Mining and Manufacturing (3M), or Federal Steel played a key role.

The first mine, the Soudan mine at Tower, started production in 1882. Even greater was the mine at Mountain Iron opened in 1892. Soon across northern Minnesota, giant steam shovels, first used on the Vermillion Range, were scooping out huge bites of iron-rich earth. This would mark the dawn of open pit iron mining, then a largely untested concept. In the 1890s, the true beginning of Minnesota iron mining, the state produced 43 million tons of ore, a staggering amount at the time. In the next decade, the total jumped to 208 million tons. By the 1930s, two thirds of all iron ore in the U.S. came from Minnesota. During both world wars, almost unbelievable amounts of ore were mined. From 1940 to 1945, 338 million tons was pulled from the ground. Via great iron-ore carry ships, Minnesota's mineral wealth fueled the forges and foundries of Cleveland, Youngstown, Chicago, and Pittsburgh during the greatest period of industrial growth in American history.

The engine of Minnesota's expansion, particularly on the farming frontier but also in timber and iron, was the railroad. It is impossible to overestimate the impact of the railroad on the history of this era. It was more than just a means of getting goods and people from one place to another. The train was the symbol of progress and modernity. It transformed how people thought about space and time. (Indeed, the whole notion of "standard time" was a product of the railroad.) Being connected to the railroad was to become part of a glittering new world of science, industry, and "progress." Nor was this great symbol of modernity something one could see only in the largest and most advanced cities, for the railroad could also be a feature of life in the smallest and newest towns of the western prairies and northern forests. Having a railroad made small-town denizens feel connected, modern, and up-to-date. By the 1880s, the metropolis of Chicago was but a few days journey from the most remote reaches of western Minnesota.

The railroad did more than just transport; it also built. Settlement in pre-Civil War Minnesota had followed the line of the state's major rivers. St. Paul, Minneapolis, Hastings, Winona, Stillwater, St. Peter, Mankato, and New Ulm were all located on rivers and could be served by steamboats. By the 1860s, however, the limits of navigable river courses in Minnesota had been reached. Some towns, like Redwood Falls (near the site of the Lower Sioux Agency), were accessible by boat only part of the summer and fall due to variable river levels. When the river froze in the winter, no barge traffic was possible anywhere and if there was a drought and water levels dropped, the boats had great difficulty. So the railroad was the only real alternative for profitable settlement and expansion.

But railroads cannot make money by running track through uninhabited land, and without people to grow and ship gain. Some means was needed to induce private companies to build lines in areas with few people. Recognizing this, the state of Minnesota, as well as some municipalities and counties, did all in their power to promote railroads, as did the federal government on the national level. Given the relative lack of cash in the American government, the primary method of doing such promotion was to provide land grants. The Winona and St. Peter Railroad, owned by the Chicago and North Western after 1867, received every odd-numbered section in nearly every township in southwestern Minnesota and eastern South Dakota. The idea was that the railroad could finance its construction into these regions by selling off its land grants to prospective settlers.

So it was the railroad that determined the human landscape of much of western Minnesota. It sited towns more or less six miles apart. (Three miles and back was theoretically the round trip a farmer with a wagon load of grain could make—leaving time to shop and pick up mail in town—and still get home for evening chores before dark.) This arrangement also helped ensure that competing railroad lines did not sneak their own branch line in between two widely-spaced towns and steal business. Having a monopoly on shipping in and out of a particular area was a real advantage.

Nor was that all. The railroads also arranged the town plans to suit their needs. Key railroad installation and the all important stockyards and grain elevators were sited along the tracks. To minimize crossing of the tracks, all development was placed on the right side of the rail line. Less crossing of tracks meant fewer accidents, which delayed trains and cut down on profitability. (This also created a less-developed area that could become home to transients, hoboes, and others who lived on the "wrong side of the tracks.")

Each town was virtually identical to the other. This was true throughout much of western and southern Minnesota, as well as right across the Great Plains from Texas to southern Canada. In a hundred towns the visitor can go to the corner of First and Main and look left and see a bank (or where a bank used to be). Business lots were small, so more could be sold. Each town was envisioned as having a full range of small businesses, despite the fact that each of its neighbors (six miles away) had exactly the same arrangement.

Wherever the railroad went, land prices rose, so speculators were constantly trying to out-guess the railroad and buy up land and found towns ahead of the tracks. One speculator even put his buildings on sleds that could be hitched to teams of oxen so he could quickly relocate. Other small towns were founded by local settlers, often of a particular immigrant group, who came together to build a church and open a post office. In nearly all cases, the railroad deliberately bypassed these pre-existing town sites and built a new town, often less than a mile away, which in most cases caused the earlier town to fold. Railroads made no profit by running a line though a town that already existed.

Railroads were loved and hated by Minnesotans of the late nineteenth century. Farmers and merchants who did not have a nearby railroad were constantly petitioning railroad companies to build additional branch lines. At the same time, these companies charged whatever price the market could bear. They frequently owned all the grain elevators and were the only ones to whom farmers could sell their grain. Railroad companies also tried to dictate where local business could buy bulk goods, such as coal. The Chicago and North Western often tried to keep merchants in small towns, where the C&NW was the sole line, from shipping their grain to cities other than Chicago and from buying bulk goods from any place but Chicago. In the small town of Minneota, for example, the newspaper reported: "Martin Furgeson, of the Independent Grain company told us that Mr. Weston also wished to know where he [Furgeson] shipped his grain, and being told that most of it went to Minneapolis and some to Chicago, wanted to know why he could not ship it all to Chicago.

Martin asked whether the railroad intended to dictate as to that also, and was told that it was to come next." When they were not demanding more or better rail service, local farmers and merchants were organizing protests against the railroad companies and their monopolistic practices.

THE GREAT SETTLEMENT

Despite problems with the railroad, for the landless immigrant seeking a farm, the journeyman who wanted to be the master of his own shop, or the entrepreneur with dreams of starting a new business, there was no better opportunity than Minnesota's rural frontier. The dream was that, through hard work and endurance, they could make a better life for themselves and, more importantly, for their children. Hardship would claim many, but for many more this frontier was a ticket to something better and was indeed, God's country.

The settlers came, sometimes individuals (even single women), but more often families. They arrived in a river port or rail station with their worldly goods, tools, and animals (or with enough money saved up to buy what was needed). By covered wagon they went out to stake their claim. Even a poor family could lay claim to 160 acres of land under the Homestead Act, provided they could tough it out for the necessary five years. Others took tree claims, promising to plant a certain number of trees. As good homestead land became more scarce, settlers purchased land from railroad companies or speculators who made a living buying up failed claims.

As settlers poured in, a wave of heady optimism created a whole language of boosterism on display in hundreds of small-town newspapers. In 1869, the *Redwood Falls Patriot* exclaimed:

> The grand rush into this County has commenced, and already, some 150 families have arrived, while hundreds of stranger[s] without their families, are looking out for homes. We are glad to see them coming. The day will soon come when Redwood County will boast a population of 50,000 people. Redwood Falls is the center of attraction and proposes to be the mistress of trade in Western Minnesota.

Modern grain elevators, Minneapolis

Every railroad siding was promoted as the next Chicago. Town plans that showed grids of streets, grand parks, and other amenities were more often wishful thinking than reality. Settlers arrived to find surveyors' stakes instead of streets. Whether the new communities became boom towns or ghost towns, it was up to the settlers to make the dreams of the boosters a reality.

Neither the state nor the railroads were willing to simply wait for settlers to arrive. Each company and the state itself (often working in concert) set up immigration bureaus and published pamphlets and placed newspaper ads to attract settlers. These circulated not only in the United States but also in Canada and throughout Europe. Local ethnic newspapers were eager to translate promotional materials into their native languages to attract more settlers from the homeland to Minnesota. The state opened a special office in Quebec to assist newly arrived Norwegian immigrants in choosing the North Star State.

Railroads, ethnic organizations, and churches also worked together to establish special religious or ethnic colonies. Archbishop John Ireland of St. Paul was particularly zealous in seeking to build rural Irish communities and save his compatriots from the perils of life in America's new industrial cities. When the idea was met with a lukewarm response, Ireland turned to other Catholic groups: Germans, French, Belgians, and Poles. The Danish Evangelical Lutheran Church, interested in creating all-Danish colonies, also struck a deal with the railroad, which set aside some 35,000 acres in western Minnesota for Danes. Although some of these efforts were successful, others were not. A few were legally questionable and left a bad aftertaste and resentments within some ethnic communities. An early Czech-language history castigates a fellow Czech immigrant who bought up large parcels of land near the town of Hopkins and sold them at a huge profit to fellow immigrants. A pair of Polish promoters who unsuccessfully tried to sell land in southern Minnesota with supposedly valuable mineral deposits to their compatriots was later arrested in Wisconsin for defrauding their fellow immigrants in another shady colonization scheme.

In the age of wheat, some wealthy investors took advantage of cheap land to create huge "bonanza" farms of

20,000 or 30,000 acres. By 1895 St. Paul lawyer Oliver Dalrymple owned 100,000 acres in the Red River valley with 65,000 acres under cultivation. Historian Theodore Blegen notes: "A humble worker on Dalrymple's bonanza farm in 1887 was the later Nobel Prize winner Knut Hamsun. To him the prairie was 'golden-green and endless as a sea.' He drove one of ten mowing machines in harvest, working sixteen hours a day; men followed the machines to shock the wheat bundles. The scene was 'wheat and grass, wheat and grass, as far as the eye could see.'"

Most farms were much smaller, cut out of the tough prairie sod, with the sod used to create warm if crude dugouts—the proverbial sod house. In areas with enough wood, the pioneers could build a crude log cabin, often without even the luxury of windows. Martha Thorne, who settled with her family in Blue Earth County, remembered their first home:

> Such a beautiful spot it was, this home spot! We camped for three weeks, living in our prairie schooner, while the men put up the wild hay.... We built a log cabin with "chinkins" to let in the air. We filled in the cracks except where these chinkins were, with mud. The roof was made by laying popple poles so they met over the middle and fastening them together. Over this we laid a heavy thickness of wild hay, and over that the popple poles again well tied with hand twisted ropes to those below. It was a good roof, only it leaked like a sieve. The floor was just the ground. Over it we put a layer of wild hay and then staked a rag carpet over it.

Men, women, and children worked day and night. Even children as young as four or five would tend geese or cattle, or take care of chickens. Mary Weeks, who came to Minnesota with her husband in 1853, recalled:

> I used to do all the housework for a family of seven besides making butter and taking care of the chickens. If help was short, I helped with the milking, too. I made all the clothes the men wore. A tailor would cut out their suits and then I would make them by hand. I made all the shirts, too. You should have seen the fancy bosumed shirts I made. Then I knit stocking and mittens for the whole family and warm woolen scarfs

for their necks. My husband used to go to bed tired to death and leave me sitting up working. He always hated to leave me. Then he would find me up no matter how early it was. He said I never slept. I didn't have much time to waste that way. We lived on beautiful Silver Lake. In season the pink lady-slippers grew in great patches and other flowers to make the prairie gay.

There was little in the way of comfort and those who could not "do for themselves" or who got sick were lost. Martha Thorne told an interviewer many years later: "My baby was born three weeks after we moved in. There was no doctor for a hundred miles. I got through, helped only by my sister-in-law. What do you women nowadays, with your hospitals and doctors, know of a time like this?"

It is hard to underestimate the hardship endured by the state's early pioneers. "How little those who enjoy this state now think what it cost the makers of it!" remarked one early settler. Prairie and forest fires were a constant menace in the dry summer months. On the prairie, the sky would first darken with the smoke and then a line of flame could often be seen all along the horizon, driven by the west wind. If they had time, the settlers could race to plow a circle around their farmstead in the hope of creating a fire break that would at least save their buildings and gardens. If the fire came on too fast, they could run to a nearby creek or slough and submerge themselves and their children, leaving only their faces above water. Those who lived in sod dugouts might survive wrapped in wet blankets if the fire moved quickly enough. Many times, though, whole families could be lost, burnt alive or suffocated as the fire consumed the very air in their lungs.

Another threat came in the winter. If today the state's mythic winters are a mere nuisance and a cause for the occasional quip about the weather, in the late nineteenth century and well into the twentieth century blizzards killed many people. With driving snow and wind chills as low as -50°F, those caught out in the open or unprepared could quickly die of exposure. In an age before reliable weather forecasts, this was quite common, and once the snow and wind started it was impossible to determine directions or distances. A farmer could freeze walking from his house to his barn if, in the white-out, he missed the barn and walked

Famous Minnesotans: James J. Hill

Born Sept. 16, 1838, Rockwood, Ontario. Died May 29, 1916, St. Paul.

James Jerome Hill was the quintessential American "rail baron." Starting with limited capital and a small railroad, Hill built one of North America's biggest railroad empires, for which he received the title "the Empire Builder." As a young man, Hill re-located to St. Paul, then known primarily as the northernmost river port on the Mississippi. He later built up enough capital to go into business with a friend, operating steam boats on the Red River. In 1878 he and three partners bought the bankrupt St. Paul and Pacific Railroad. Within a few years, Hill had turned the railroad around, renamed it the Great Northern, and by 1893 pushed his lines all the way to Puget Sound. The original "hands-on" manager, Hill oversaw most aspects of the business and was an almost obsessive workaholic. He also acquired other railroads through outright purchase (the Northern Pacific and the Chicago, Burlington and Quincy), formed many subsidiaries (such as the Minnesota and Manitoba), and was an important organizer of the Canadian Pacific Railroad. The press sometimes castigated Hill for his monopolistic tactics due to his responsibility, in part, for the severe overbuilding of rail lines and towns in several areas (notably North Dakota). Yet he was also a pioneer in promoting conservation and supporting national parks.

out into the prairie. (To prevent this, it was common to stretch a rope between the buildings to hold on to.) As the daughter of one pioneer advised, more people would have survived blizzards if they had trusted their horses and oxen. "A horse will make it home," she said. Those who survived being caught out in a snow storm frequently lost fingers, toes, noses, or ears to frostbite. Still people coped. The daughter recalled her father walking 30 miles through the snow to bring a 50-pound sack of flour back home to feed his family.

Although it was a rare winter that did not have at least one major storm, some winters live on in memory for their epic ferocity. Perhaps the worst was the winter of 1880/81, which was immortalized in *The Long Winter* by Laura

Ingalls Wilder. In southwest Minnesota, where the Wilders lived, fourteen major blizzards and countless smaller storms struck the region. As one local historian wrote: "Blizzard followed blizzard. The railroads were blockaded for weeks and months at a time. Fuel and food were nearly exhausted. People burned green wood, fences, lumber, hay, and grain and went without lights. In some places there was suffering for lack of food." Isolated towns organized gangs of men with spades to try to clear mile after mile of railroad tracks in an often futile effort to reopen the lines. Snow was piled so high that livestock were trapped inside barns and farmers had to cut holes in barn roofs to get food inside. Some families spent days in bed to conserve food and warmth. In April 1881, a sudden warm spell ended winter's blast and created floods that washed away the newly re-opened rail lines.

If facing such annual troubles was not bad enough, the state was also visited by special plagues. The most devastating were the grasshopper plagues of the mid 1870s. The first infestation arrived in the summer of 1873. Near Lynd, a party of picnickers was enjoying a sunny day when a cloud seemed to darken the sky. The great cloud looked like a "sheet of dull silver." Some thought the specks were fluffy cottonwood seeds. The cloud circled around and around and gradually descended toward the ground and the picnickers fled. Their story was at first met with skepticism, so a party from a nearby town went out to investigate:

> When they reached the Redwood River their progress was stopped. The horse refused to approach… and there before them, covering a space twenty rods wide and for a considerable distance along the bank, the locusts were piled up two inches deep, a moving, undulating mass animation. The insects had there piled by the million and where they covered stumps and brush they gave the appearance of being several feet deep.

There was no rhyme or reason to the attack. Some areas were stripped bare, gardens and crops eaten away so completely it was as if someone had taken a knife to every plant and cut it off at the roots, while neighboring areas might remain untouched. Massive swarms of grasshoppers swept in, laid eggs, ate everything, and left. The history of Lyon County records:

Parts of the county were literally alive with the voracious insects. So thick was the air with the flying pests that at times the sun was obscured…. At evening when they came down near the earth, the noise they made was like a roaring wind. Those that alighted on the prairies seemed to know where the grain field and gardens were and gathered in them from all directions. Every cornstalk was bent to the earth with their weight. The noise they made eating could be heard from quite a distance…. After gorging themselves with the crops, the grasshoppers sometimes piled up in the fields and along roads to a depth of one or two feet. Horses could not be driven through them. Stories are told of railway trains becoming blockaded by the pests so as to be unable to move.

The response of some people was of complete denial. More than one small-town newspaper did not print a single word about the infestation destroying their communities. State and local governments gave aid slowly and in quantities too small to alleviate the problem. In some towns, the destitute were required to stand up in a public meeting and list all their assets to prove they were truly needy. For many proud settlers who had come west to be independent, it was too much to ask. Many simply abandoned their claims and left the region.

Added to this were the threats of diseases such as cholera and scarlet fever, which could wipe out whole families in just days. More than one newspaper listed deaths of children in a single family on successive days. Health care was virtually non-existent. Working with farm animals and sharp tools resulted in numerous accidents.

Finally, there was the isolation that drove many to the point of madness. Although it affected both men and women, the strain was particularly hard on women. While men were often traveling to work and gone for days at a time, women were left at home either alone or to care for a house full of children. For those who had grown up in tightly knit villages in Europe or in small towns and cities elsewhere in America, the strain was enormous.

Even in normal times, ordinary bad luck or bad planning led to an up and down cycle for many of the early settlers. A. P. Connolly tried his hand at a homestead in northwest Minnesota in the hope that he could sell his land at a profit: "All things come to an end, and so did this wild goose chase after riches…. To sum up my reward for this five months of hard work, privation, and danger, I had one red flannel short, one pair of boots, one pair white duck pants, and $13 worth of groceries. Wasn't this a jolt?"

Some were upset to find accounts penned by immigration agents misleading. One Danish immigrant wrote home to say: "Before I emigrated to America I received a description of Minnesota from the agent of the Bremen Line in Copenhagen. Everything was described in glowing terms. Among other things, the climate was supposed to be extraordinarily pleasant. The truth is that Minnesota has completely tropical summers and Siberian winters. That is hardly 'pleasant' for people who come from a temperate climate."

In spite of it all, the settlers continued to come, driven by hope. Many failed, but many more made it. Nowhere else could a landless cotter from Norway or Sweden acquire through dint of hard work 160 acres of land, more than most of the biggest landowners in their homelands. The Homestead Act was met with disbelief by some newspapers in Norway: having so much land essentially for free strained the imagination. For the immigrants in particular, while they faced hardship in the new land, they had also faced hardship at home. Here, however, a person could succeed. And while the frontier could be harsh, it could also be beautiful.

Mrs. C. A. Smith, the daughter of Swedish pioneers who settled near Chaska, recalled:

> We lived just as we had in Sweden, as we were in a Swedish settlement. We were Lutheran so there were no parties. Going to church was our only amusement…. The prairies were perfectly lovely with their wild flower setting. There had been a fire two years before and great thickets of blackberry vines had grown up. I never saw such blackberries. They were as large as the first joint of a man thumb. The flavor was wild and spicy. I never ate anything so good. Cranberries by the hundreds of bushels grew in the swamps. We could not begin to pick all the hazel nuts. We used to eat turnips as we would an apple. They were so sweet.

Spring wild flower Trillium, found in the Minnesota woods

Even the seeming isolation of life on the frontier could be overcome, as M. G. Cobb remembered:

> It seemed at first in those early days impossible to have social relations with anyone. Neighbors as we had known them, we had none.... But we soon learned that we had neighbors though the distance was considerable. First one neighbor then another would extend to every family in the vicinity an invitation to spend an afternoon or evening.... We rode and visited and sang until we reached the appointed place, where, perhaps eight, ten, or a dozen persons spent the afternoon or evening in one little room, where the meal was being prepared and the table spread. There were no sets or clans, no grades of society, all belonged to the select four hundred, and all were treated and fared alike. Friendships formed that were never broken.

There was pride, too, in making a life on the frontier. An early Czech account from Steele County notes: "The present generation can hardly imagine the very beginnings of the poor immigrants. Forest and brush were everywhere.... Anyway the Czech work ethic and patience changed the countryside very much. Beautiful houses and barns can be seen at every farm today." Polish immigrants from Lincoln County wrote their compatriots back east to say:

> The soil here is extraordinarily fertile, the water healthful and clear as crystal, and the people are free; the land provides easy sustenance to those who are willing to work on a farm and who wish for clear air and a life that is more agreeable than in the great, overcrowded cities where people work in factories.... A few years ago there was only a miserable desert here, with no schools and no church. Today in Wilno there is a church and a happy Polish settlement around it. Morning and evening the church bells ring out over the prairie, reminding the people of their distant Catholic homeland.

A Diverse State

Those who came to Minnesota were a diverse lot, arriving from many different countries and states. By 1910, in nearly every county in the state, at least half of the population were immigrants or children of immigrants, making Minnesota one of most heavily immigrant states at that time.

As was so often the case, however, native-born Yankees arrived prior to the largest immigrant waves. Their migration had begun before the Civil War and continued throughout the 1860s and 1870s. Railroads eagerly recruited them for towns (whereas German and Scandinavian immigrants were more likely to be recruited as farmers). Towns across Minnesota bear names brought from upstate New York or New England such as Little Falls, Rochester, New York Mills, Taunton, Warsaw, or Farmington. In many of the state's new small towns and cities, Yankees formed the social, economic, and political elite. They held the major public offices, both elective and appointive. They served on commissions and were elected to state and national office. Their wives made up local library boards and were leaders in school and church affairs. And they formed associations, particularly Masonic or Masonic-like organizations. Small towns and cities often had scores of these groups.

If the Yankees were the elite, then the elite of the elite were Civil War veterans. Forming local posts of the national Grand Army of the Republic (GAR) and addressing each other as "comrade," these men had the common bond of military service and the world-view shaped by the conflict between the states. They took civic duty very seriously. In many towns the local GAR post was the real center of political and social life. Memorial Day ceremonies honoring Civil War dead were elaborate, day-long spectacles with speeches and parades and none of the relaxed start-of-summer attitude common in more recent decades. The GAR posts were also usually local strongholds of the Republican party in Minnesota, which was seen by its adherents as the party of Lincoln and of progressive American values.

The Yankees also had a reputation for being highly mobile to the point of wanderlust, whether it be to pick up stakes and move to the next county for a slightly better farm or to head out for the gold fields of Colorado. Pa Ingalls, of *Little House on the Prairie* fame, was stereotypical in that he never seemed satisfied with his situation and was repeatedly moving his family to a spot where the grass would be greener. As farmers, Yankees tended to remain on the land for but a generation. Their children went to college and got white-collar jobs when possible, or the families sold their land to immigrants and moved to town to open a business.

Other groups with roots in the British Isles also arrived in Minnesota. British immigrants and British Canadians were in Minnesota already during the era of the fur trade, as were Scots and Scots-Irish. Scots entrepreneurs invested in Minnesota real estate and established some rural settlements, such as Cambria in south-central Minnesota. Welsh, Manx, and those born in various British colonies also arrived in small numbers.

The most noticeable group of immigrants from the British Isles were the Irish. The majority of these newcomers were Catholic. (Protestant Irish tended to join communities with other Protestants from the British Isles or with Yankees.) As a large, English-speaking group, the Irish played an important role in Minnesota's history. From its establishment, the Archdiocese of St. Paul and Minneapolis has always been headed by an Irish or Irish-American prelate. In the city of St. Paul, as in many eastern cities, the Irish found politics a useful avenue of advancement in American society, though they were outnumbered by other groups, such as the Germans. They formed alliances with these other groups, including Protestant Yankees, and came to dominate politics in the Saintly City and contribute such notable Minnesotans as Ignatius Donnelly.

Attempts to form rural Irish colonies never lived up to the hopes of their promoters, most notably the powerful Archbishop John Ireland. Their legacy can still be seen in a scattering of names on the map: Clontarff, Iona, or Green Isle. Although Irish in rural Minnesota formed few concentrated communities, quite a few took up farms interspersed with other ethnic groups. As an 1877 pamphlet for potential Irish settlers to Minnesota put it, "Those who own farms own the country"—a powerful appeal to a group so often disenfranchised in their own homeland. The Irish were also a significant presence in railroad construction gangs of the late nineteenth century and laid many of the track lines across the state.

French Canadians continued to be a presence in the state due to new migration from other communities, particularly Illinois. St. Paul was a major center for French Canadians and one account noted that, "for several years French Canadians were quite a large percentage of the population. A knowledge of the French tongue was almost indispensable for a tradesman then." Smaller western European groups also came, in particular Swiss, French, Dutch (naming towns like Holland), Belgians (contributing towns like Ghent), and Luxembourgers.

Minnesota's Germans were the largest single immigrant group and one of the least known. Germans arrived in the state early and continued to come through World War I and even thereafter. Today their descendants make up the state's largest ethnic group. Yet the Germans were a heterogeneous lot, divided by both faith and region. There were Catholics, Lutherans of several denominations, Methodists, Baptists, Mennonites, Jews, and the atheistic Freethinkers. They came from many regions of Germany proper, but also from regions of Austria-Hungary (especially Bohemia), and even from German minorities in Poland and Russia. Some Germans came to Minnesota directly from Europe, while others sojourned in other states before moving west. Though speaking a common tongue with a number of local dialects, these groups usually formed distinct communities.

"Minnesota receives annually thousands of German immigrants," noted one 1870 pamphlet directed at potential German immigrants. "To those who want to part with Germany we recommend German Minnesota, the most faithful likeness of the old homeland that this continent can offer, as a home." Although Germans could be found in virtually every corner of the state, the heartland of German settlement was in the center of the state from the Mankato–New Ulm–Redwood Falls area north to Fergus Falls and Brainerd, with additional concentrations in the Mississippi valley of southeast Minnesota. By 1900 there were probably at least 300,000 German immigrants in Minnesota.

Occupying some of Minnesota's richest farmland, these settlers brought large families, whose labor played a major role in making the state an agricultural giant. Although center for ethnic culture. The fraternal insurance society Sons of Norway was founded there in 1895 and soon had branches in Norwegian communities around the state and around the nation. The Norwegians were split into several religious factions, and theological controversies among Norwegian Lutherans proved bitter. Yet these disputes also led to the establishment of a variety of Lutheran colleges in Minnesota. St. Olaf in Northfield, Augsburg College in Minneapolis, and Concordia College in Moorhead are the most notable results of these divisions. Each was originally established to train young men for the ministry but in time developed into full fledged liberal arts colleges.

The educational tradition became extremely important for Norwegian immigrants, signaling a desire for their children to have a life beyond the family farm. Though more persistent on the land than Yankees, Norwegians were willing to have their children enter other professions. This became especially notable in the realm of politics, where Norwegians have done extremely well. Where other immigrant groups kept a lower profile, Norwegians took to politics with vigor. Though often conservative, like other Scandinavian groups, Norwegian Americans also exhibited a hearty streak of populism that strongly influenced state politics.

Swedish immigrants also poured into Minnesota in the decades following the Civil War, at times almost equaling the Norwegian influx. By 1890 the census recorded nearly 100,000 Swedish immigrants in the state. Unlike the Norwegians, who preferred homes and farms in the prairie regions of the western and southern parts of Minnesota, the heaviest areas of Swedish settlement were found in the eastern and central part of the state, particularly between the St. Croix and Mississippi rivers. This area, which had been logged over by lumber companies, provided less fertile soil but more timber resources. Some Swedish settlement also occurred in the west central part of the state, from Litchfield north to Fergus Falls and also in the far northwest corner of the state.

Counties like Chisago and Isanti thus became heavily Swedish. Isanti, which had a strong migration from the Dalarna region of Sweden, retained regional dialects and customs longer than in Sweden itself. One early account by a

Must-See Sites: American Swedish Institute, Minneapolis

The American Swedish Institute, founded in 1929, celebrates Swedish and Swedish-American culture. The Turnblad mansion, which houses the institute, is on the National Register of Historic Places and is the only "castle" in the Twin Cities. The museum showcases the institute's collection of Swedish glass, decorative and fine arts, textiles, and items from Sweden. A permanent exhibit explores the local Swedish-American commun-ity through photographs, diaries, vintage recordings, and immigrant artifacts.

Contact: (612) 871-4907; Web: www.americanswedishinst.org
Location: 2600 Park Avenue, Minneapolis.

Swedish Lutheran pastor recalled how the Dalarna Swedes came "to church in festive array, with clothes cut according to the ancient style, the man dressed in the inevitable leather apron, and the woman with the short waist, red stockings and large shoes."

Swedes also came in large numbers to Minnesota's cities and later to the Iron Range, working first as common laborers but soon moving into white-collar jobs as well. Both St. Paul and Minneapolis developed large Swedish commun-ities as did smaller cities and towns: Red Wing, Duluth, St. Peter, and Willmar. Areas of St. Paul and Minneapolis took on names such as Swede Hollow or Swede Alley that reflected these urban communities.

Danes also arrived in Minnesota, though not nearly as many as Swedes or Norwegians. Danes spread out widely in the state and often assimilated quickly or joined Norwegian communities. One significant exception to this were communities created by the Danish Evangelical Lutheran Church, the best known example being the Danebod community in Tyler. This community developed as a bulwark of Danish ethnicity in the state. In 1888 the community's proud pastor wrote to say:

War, by the 1880s and 1890s significant streams of new Minnesotans also arrived from eastern and southern Europe. The largest of these groups were Poles. The first Polish settlers arrived in the 1850s, but significant numbers of the Poles did not begin to arrive until the late 1870s and 1880s. Winona became a major center of Polish settlement and Polish farming communities were scattered across the state by 1900, leaving such names on the map as Wilno, Sobieski, and Opole. The largest rural concentration was in central Minnesota from St. Cloud to Little Falls. Poles also settled in large numbers in St. Paul and "Nordeast" Minneapolis as well as in Duluth and the Iron Range.

Arriving slightly earlier than the Poles, though in smaller numbers, were Czech immigrants. The best-known Czech settlement is New Prague in Scott County, though many small Czech settlements are found throughout southern and central Minnesota. Both Twin Cities developed Czech communities as well. Other significant Slavic groups in the state include Slovaks (who settled in Minneapolis), Ukrainians, and Carpatho-Rusins. South Slavic groups, particularly Serbs, Croatians, and Slovenes, settled in South St. Paul and were a major presence in northern Minnesota's iron mines. Hungarians, Romanians, Lithuanians, Latvians, and Estonians came in smaller numbers to the Twin Cities. Each of these groups developed its own distinctive ethnic institutions, such as churches, periodicals, and mutual aid societies.

Jewish immigrants arrived from eastern Europe by the end of the nineteenth century, mainly from the Russian empire but also from Austria-Hungary and Germany. The largest concentration was in North Minneapolis, but a Jewish community also sprung up in St. Paul. Less well-known, however, is the fact that Jews were also present in many of the state's smaller rural towns, first as peddlers and later as established Main Street businesspeople. Most of their enterprises were modest, but a few grew to prominence, whether through luck or sheer entrepreneurial pluck. One example was the Wiener family of Marshall, which parlayed small-time junk-buying into a major agricultural processing and wholesale business. By the 1940s, the family's Marshall Produce plant was the world's largest producer of dried eggs.

From southern Europe came Greeks and Italians, both of whom settled primarily in urban areas and on the Iron Range, though scattered bands of each group were also occasionally found in more rural areas. Although most early migrants were laborers, both groups found commercial niches, such as peddling or opening small restaurants, some of which would eventually become quite noteworthy. Roma (Gypsies) were often seen traveling about rural areas of the state, though little is known about their presence in Minnesota.

Other migrants and immigrants came from other regions of North America and other parts of the world. African Americans had lived in Minnesota since its days as a territory, and their numbers prior to Emancipation included both slaves brought by traveling slave owners and free African Americans. In the early Minnesota censuses, the majority of African Americans were described as being people of mixed race. Both St. Paul and Minneapolis developed small African American communities by the 1880s, and the first African-American newspaper in the state, *The Western Appeal*, was founded in 1885, though it soon moved to the east. African Americans in outstate Minnesota tended to be fairly transient, working stints in local hotels as entertainers and even as "ringers" for small-town baseball teams.

The growth of African American communities in the Twin Cities increased after World War I with laws that cut off east European immigration. African Americans began to move north to escape the more extreme racial prejudice of the South, yet they could not escape it comletely. In 1931 an African American war veteran and postal worker provoked a near-riot when he moved his family into an all white neighborhood in South Minneapolis. The family received police protection and much public support and ultimately stayed. Nevertheless, such progress was slow and there were clear racial boundaries for housing, furthered by restrictive housing covenants.

African Americans also faced restrictions in employment. Many of the first African American businessmen were barbers. The Twin Cities were also home to many African American railroad porters. These jobs, while often menial, were better than what could be had in the South. Yet African Americans were effectively barred

Minnesota in the decades after the Civil War and statehood had in common the desire for a better life and the need to be at home in Minnesota. This meant more than simply trying to recreate what had existed back in one's old home or in the old country. It meant creating something entirely new, a hybrid that mixed tradition with new forms. Rather than choose to live as Norwegian or American, or German or American, they chose to live as Norwegian and American, as Germans and American.

Many immigrants arrived without a strong sense of national identity. Their primary loyalties were to family, village, and church (or synagogue). Lack of economic opportunity and social barriers kept many from participating in national life and national culture in their homelands. Some groups, such as Poles, Jews, or Lithuanians, had been denied significant national expression under the German, Russian, or Austro-Hungarian empires. Most Norwegians arrived prior to Norway's full independence from Sweden in 1905. In their new Minnesota homes, these immigrants learned about the countries they had left behind and had the opportunity to read national literature and listen to national composers. Ironically, they often learned more about their homelands in America than they had before immigration.

Their new Minnesota homes not only provided economic opportunity but also a chance for immigrants to express themselves in ways that had not been possible before. One result of this was a kind of cultural explosion. Minnesota became home to scores of foreign-language newspapers and book and music publishers, all of whom catered to a specific ethnic market of fellow immigrants. These newcomers wrote literature, recited poems, composed and performed music, painted, and developed new forms of vernacular and religious architecture. Minneapolis architect Wiktor Kordela exemplified this new spirit. Half-Polish, half-Italian, and educated in western Ukraine, Kordela designed churches for German, Polish, Slovak, Ukrainian, and Carpatho-Rusin communities all across Minnesota and Wisconsin that combined familiar Old World elements, such as onion domes, with New World materials and forms. These churches became the stone and mortar roots that bound the immigrants to their new homes.

The immigrants' sense of what it meant to be an American developed gradually, but their loyalty to their new local settings was immediate. They became Minnesotans, St. Paulites, or Alexandrians before they became Americans. They joined and followed local sports teams (often with detailed accounts in their own language). They paid close attention to local elections. They wrote poems and songs extolling the virtues of their new communities and bragged about the advantages of Minnesota to compatriots elsewhere.

Just as the immigrants worked to remake themselves with new identities in a new home, the native-born Anglo-Americans underwent a parallel process. The arrival of so many immigrants caused these Minnesotans to more clearly define who they were and what it meant to be American. American came to mean someone who spoke English without a "foreign" accent and whose ancestors came from the British Isles. Old Settler Associations, GAR posts and their auxiliaries, and Masonic organizations all helped in this process. So, too, did the summer Chautauqua, a combination of education, entertainment, and moral uplift that became a common feature of small Yankee communities in the decades prior to the arrival of the motion picture and the radio.

Each of these groups, immigrants, and migrants formed distinct communities with their own religions, languages, and customs. They interacted in the marketplace and the stores where English—often poorly spoken—became the lingua franca between immigrants from a dozen different countries. Intermarriage was infrequent, and when it did occur it was usually among groups who spoke a common or closely related language and had a common religion.

Cultural misunderstandings and mutual prejudice were common, as one might expect when so many diverse groups arrive in one location. Aside from fights at dances or saloons over who was dating whom, serious conflicts were rare, at least until World War I. In 1905, for example, Czech and Norwegian youths in Hansonville township of Lincoln County began a brawl over who would get into a local dance. The incident was more sound than fury, but this did not stop a local newspaper from leading off with the headline "Race

War in Hansonville." Old country politics provided an occasional opportunity for conflict as well.

More serious differences occurred over politics, religion, or some combination of the two. Early Protestant Scandinavian and German communities fought frequent doctrinal battles, the Lutherans, in particular experiencing internal conflict. Catholics, the state's largest domination, also had their tensions. The Irish Catholic hierarchy sought to "Americanize" groups like Germans, Ukrainians, and Poles, which those groups felt meant making them over to be as much like the Irish as possible. The powerful Archbishop John Ireland bitterly resented the strong and independent German Benedictine community at St. John's in central Minnesota, which provided a spiritual and cultural counterweight for the state's German Catholics. A conflict with a local Ukrainian Catholic priest sparked a mass conversion to Russian Orthodoxy that soon spread to many Ukrainian and Carpatho-Rusin communities around the country.

For the most part, Minnesotans accepted their neighbors from other lands and with other beliefs and cultures, even though it took a few generations of living together in the same place for serious barriers to break down.

One group that continued to have trouble finding its place in this new, multicultural Minnesota, however, were the descendants of the state's first inhabitants. The state's expelled Dakota were scattered across the west and even into Canada, but did not forget Minnesota. In the early 1880s, small groups of Christian Dakota actually returned to a few small reservations in southern Minnesota, a migration whose story has not been adequately documented. In the north, the Ojibwe had been bypassed by the troubles of the 1860s, but the growth of logging, mining, and the expansion of settlement, eventually forced them onto reservations. These reservations were then gradually constricted. The Ojibwe were promised many things by the government, but, as had happened to the Dakota, these promises were often not honored due to incompetence or ill-will.

In 1889 the government attempted to liquidate some of the reservations and give each Ojibwe family a farm. Naturally, this did not sit well with many Native

Americans. As one government report notes, "The commissioners did not escape the embarrassment which unfortunately too often attends our negotiations with the Indians, viz.: An indisposition to further treat with the Government while its obligations incurred under former agreements are unkept." Transcripts of the negotiations reveal that the Ojibwe had started to learn how to deal with the government, for the matter of the government's unkept promises was raised again and again. They also reveal deep divisions within each community, particularly with tribal members of mixed race and families where some members had intermarried with whites. One Objiwe leader at White Earth, Wob-oh-ah-quod, told the commissioners who had been sent there to secure their agreement how some were able to cheat the system and get more aid:

> Those who talk best get the [government] seed grain first, and many is the time the Indian... who through his own energy has got a little land plowed, receives no seed, while those who do not need it get it all. That happened many times.... It is issued to our sons-in-law instead of going to Indians. I mean whites who are intermarried with our families. They are the ones who can ask the most readily. They have no hesitation in asking, and we find those things given to those who are most persevering in begging; those are our sons-in-law.... Now who ought to have the preference? Is it not the Indian who first owned the soil? He ought to come first and others afterward. That is the way we view it. I am laying these facts before the commissioners in the presence of the agent, as we have heard that he was a man so partial to justice.

Much of the "excess" Native American land was sold to timber companies, and of all the northern reservations, only Red Lake remained in its original form. To add insult to injury, many Native American children were taken from their families and sent to boarding school in a failed effort to integrate Native Americans into the mainstream.

The resentments that sprang from these policies helped to fuel Minnesota's last violent conflict with its original inhabitants. In 1898, continuing tensions over timber rights and arrests of local Native Americans led a group of Leech

Lake Ojibwe to free two compatriots arrested for allegedly selling illegal liquor. A company of 100 soldiers was sent to apprehend the group near Sugar Point on Leech Lake. The soldiers, mostly raw recruits, were unable to find the Ojibwe they were looking for, though a group of armed Native Americans was watching the soldiers from the cover of the woods. When one soldier accidentally discharged his rifle, gunfire broke out. A three-hour firefight ensued and six soldiers were killed, including the company commander. Ojibwe losses were unknown. The soldiers withdrew with their dead and wounded and the Native Americans melted into the woods. A brief furor ensued and the National Guard was sent in to the area in force, though no more resistance occurred. A few Native Americans were accused of participating in the battle but received only minor sentences. The last shooting battle in Minnesota's Native American wars was, ironically, a victory for the Native Americans.

AMERICANIZATION

At the turn of the century, Minnesota was a multicultural state. Its people lived in a variety of ethnic enclaves, speaking both English and a plethora of other languages, following their own customs and faiths. Yet this multiculturalism proved to be a victim of larger forces. As "American" came to be defined more and more as English-speaking, northern and western European in origin, and Protestant, an undercurrent of tension mounted, particularly after the Spanish-American War. Old-stock Americans felt increasingly threatened by waves of new immigrants from eastern and southern Europe, particularly the large Catholic populations.

Both reactionaries and progressive reformers had their reasons to oppose foreigners and immigration, whether for nationalistic reasons or for reasons of social and cultural "hygiene." Minnesota, and particularly Minneapolis, with its strong progressive tradition tended toward the latter.

These tensions came to a head in World War I. When the U.S. declared war on Germany in April 1917, a frenzy of anti-foreign and especially anti-German feeling swept the country. Prior to the war, Germany and Germans were viewed as friendly, cultured people. Many women's study clubs in Minnesota included heavy doses of German literature and scholarly works in their self-education programs. After the war, the Germans were seen as vicious "Huns," cruel barbarians and enemies of freedom and of all that America stood for. German communities, who just a few years before had proudly proclaimed their heritage and even raised money for the German and Austrian Red Cross hospitals, suddenly became a target. All things German were banned: German books, German composers, teaching German as a foreign language in schools, even the speaking of German in public and private institutions such as churches. German Americans were harassed, attacked, sometimes even killed. Needless to say there was never any evidence that German Americans were disloyal or un-American.

Minnesota, with its large German immigration, became a hotbed of anti-German feeling. Committees of Public Safety were set up at the state and local level to monitor patriotism and to ferret out "disloyalty," which could include anything from being a pacificist to not buying enough war bonds. In New Ulm, three local officials were summarily suspended from office due to suspicions of disloyalty. Foreign-language newspapers had to submit translations of their war-related articles to the commission for approval.

Many otherwise law-abiding citizens were anony-mously denounced to the commission by their neighbors, and within German communities individuals were often willing to denounce their own compatriots. One man sent the commission a list of his neighbors from Le Sueur County and added a note: "I am German born, like the German people, but hate the German government.... take some step to check the Pro-German activities in and about Le Sueur.... Please do not expose my name at present." In some communities, ugly scenes occurred. The daughter of a German immigrant businessman from Redwood Falls recalled how someone splashed yellow paint on her father's business (yellow being the symbol of cowardice and treachery). "It broke his heart," she said. "He always considered himself an American." In Hendricks, when Armistice was declared in November 1918, a mob dragged a local family suspected of being "pro-German" from their home and publicly forced them to kiss the flag.

After the war, the state's vibrant German communities went into decline. The speaking of German and other foreign

languages decreased as parents tried to spare their children the pain of seeming "foreign" by refusing to teach them their native language. Even groups who were not German suffered, such as the Dutch, whose language sounded enough like German to stimulate sporadic discrimination as well.

The wave of anti-foreign feeling did not abate in 1918. Immigration of "undesirable" eastern and southern Europeans was restricted by law in 1924. (Immigration from Mexico was not, and as result a small Mexican community emerged in St. Paul in the 1920s.) Anti-Catholicism and anti-Semitism became more widespread, and Minneapolis emerged as a center for both. It was the headquarters of the anti-Catholic American Protective League. In addition, the city also developed the dubious distinction of being "the capital of American anti-Semitism." Jews were informally kept out of many public and private institutions, including auto clubs and golf courses. In the 1920s, small Ku Klux Klan chapters sprung up in many parts of the state. Their main target was the state's large Catholic population, and they held marches and cross burnings in front of Catholic churches as well as other protests, such as when the building materials for a new church in one small town were tossed into a local lake.

Perhaps the most notorious incident was the lynching of three young African American men in Duluth in June 1920. A city with only a very small African American community, Duluth had been prey to increasing racial resentment when U.S. Steel used imported African American workers to break a growing union effort. In the context of the post-war economic downturn and unemployment, this action helped build up fuel for a conflagration. The spark that set it off was an allegation that a group of African American circus roustabouts had raped a young white woman. A mob of at least 5,000 people broke into the local jail and seized three of six African American suspects and hung them from a lamp post. The truth about the case may never be known, but it seems likely that no rape had occurred. The incident left a stain on Duluth's reputation and there was widespread revulsion at the brutal act not only nationally and statewide but in Duluth as well. Although an isolated incident, the lynchings demonstrate the human penchant for violence, even in relatively prosperous and law-abiding places.

Expressions of intolerance always occurred side by side with good relations. Neither attitude was dominant, or at least dominant for long, and incidents like the Duluth lynching were very rare and widely deplored by most Minnesotans. By the late 1920s, what support existed for the KKK fell apart as the Klan was rocked by national scandals. Nevertheless, the state's image as a tolerant, progressive, and homogenous place that did not experience the ethnic tensions that were common elsewhere came later and only existed due to a kind of social amnesia.

7

MILLER TO AMERICA AND QUEEN OF THE RAILS: URBAN MINNESOTA

The development of the rural sectors of the state paralleled the development of Minnesota's cities, especially Minneapolis and St. Paul. As an urban conglomeration, the Twin Cities occupy a unique position in America. They have a larger hinterland—about one tenth of the entire United States—than any other urban center. This hinterland extends from western Wisconsin and upper Michigan across Minnesota and northern Iowa, all of the Dakotas, and eastern Montana. This is what geographer John Borchert called "America's northern heartland," a region dominated economically and culturally by the Twin Cities. With no other major urban centers in this large area, the Twin Cities' rise to prominence was fueled by the human and natural resources it could draw from its hinterland.

The story of how this came to be is first and foremost about transportation. As the effective northern terminus of the navigable Mississippi, eastern Minnesota marks the transition from a region that could rely on regular river traffic to a region that could not. America expanded westward, but its central river systems, with the partial exception of the Missouri, largely flow north–south. West of the Mississippi, the land grows increasingly arid. Thus, railroads became a necessity. Due to its geographic position and by virtue of its early founding as an American outpost, the Twin Cities emerged as a natural gateway between the east and the northwest.

THE INDUSTRIAL BOOM

By the 1880s, the city of St. Paul had become a major rail hub. It collected timber, grain, and other farm products from its hinterland to ship east to fuel the growth of American industry and brought in immigrants and manufactured goods to ensure continued expansion of agriculture and manufacturing. By the turn of the century, the Midway area of St. Paul (so-called because it was midway between downtown St. Paul and Minneapolis), was home to the 200-acre Minnesota Transfer station. This huge rail clearing house—the largest in the nation—was essential to managing east–west rail traffic. By 1910 a thousand men moved over half a million rail cars, or more than 1,500 a day, through this depot.

The growth of the city as a rail center was also due in no small part to late nineteenth-century America's best-known "rail baron," James J. Hill, whose Great Northern and subsidiary lines became the arteries of commerce. Hill was born in Ontario of Scottish stock and at a young age established himself in the shipping business in St. Paul. Early on, Hill saw the importance that railroads would play in the creation of the northern U.S. By 1878 he had acquired the controlling interest in the anemic St. Paul and Pacific. Using proceeds from land grants, Hill dramatically expanded his railroad, laying the basis for the Great Northern. He expanded track lines, encouraged immigration into his lands, and developed the art of managing a railroad. By 1893, the Great Northern extended from St. Paul all the way to Seattle. Hill's railroad was responsible for laying thousands of miles of track and establishing hundreds of towns, earning the nickname "the empire builder."

The expansion of the Great Northern prefigured the direction of the Twin Cities' economic and cultural hinterland and made the cities a national transport hub and the natural place for the location of industries needed to process farm products. And in the late nineteenth century, the biggest farm product was wheat. Minneapolis had developed from a grist mill at the Falls of St. Anthony. New milling technologies, first developed in Hungary, were introduced by C. A. Washburn in the 1870s, allowing the use of steel, which was better suited to Minnesota's spring wheat than the old sandstone rollers. This produced a better-tasting, more nutritious flour that was also cheaper to produce and had a longer shelf life.

Famous Minnesotans:
F. Scott Fitzgerald

Born Sept. 24, 1896, St. Paul.
Died Dec. 21, 1940, Hollywood, Calif.

One of America's best-known writers, F. Scott Fitzgerald was born to a wealthy though somewhat unstable family. His early years were spent on Summit Avenue in St. Paul, though the family moved frequently. After an unsuccessful stint at Princeton, Fitzgerald enlisted in the U.S. Army and in 1918, while stationed in Alabama, met his future wife, Zelda Sayre. Known as the chronicler of the Jazz Age, Fitzgerald's most memorable work was *The Great Gatsby*, a portrait of life among the idle rich. Its fame rests on excellent characterization and carefully drawn class distinctions between those who inherited money and those who earned it. The best-known couple of the flapper era, the Fitzgeralds gradually destroyed themselves through heavy drinking, spending sprees, and partying across two continents. Zelda was plagued by mental illness and spent the last decade of her life in institutions. Although none of Fitzgerald's other works of short or long fiction achieved the acclaim of *The Great Gatsby*, his other notable works include the novels *Tender is the Night* and *The Last Tycoon* (which was published posthumously). All three of these novels were made into movies. Fitzgerald died in 1940 of a heart attack.

One by one, mills sprung up along the Mississippi River as grain flowed in by rail and river and flour flowed out by the same paths. In 1878, Minneapolis produced 1 million barrels of flour a year. By 1902 it produced 16.3 million barrels. At that time, its nearest competitor was Milwaukee, which produced 2 million barrels a year. Even after other cities, such as Buffalo, became major milling centers, it was often thanks to investment by Minnesota's milling giants. In addition to Washburn-Crosby, with its signature product Gold Medal Flour (a company renamed as General Mills in 1928), other giants emerged, such as Pillsbury.

Washburn-Crosby and its rival Pillsbury built their early success on technological innovation. This began with the process Washburn developed to make cheap high-quality flour from spring wheat that could compete with flour made from winter wheat. Other technological advances soon followed. Mills were redesigned to allow a continuous flow of operation. They also became safer, with new ventilation that cut down on the flammable dust that was a by-product of milling, thereby helping to prevent explosions, such as the one in May 1878 that destroyed the Minneapolis Washburn mill. The net result of these changes was a product that greatly undersold all competitors and Minneapolis mills rapidly gained a dominant market share. As the city's two major milling firms sought to outdo each other, they also became innovators in marketing and in developing new wheat-based products (such as breakfast cereals) to sell to the consumer. From this beginning came such icons of marketing as Wheaties and the Pillsbury Doughboy.

As a major terminal for grain and with a large German-American community, the Twin Cities also became an important brewing center. Minneapolis and St. Paul were never as famous for beer as Milwaukee and St. Louis, but brands such as Hamms and Grain Belt helped build a large industry. Many smaller towns, such as Winona and New Ulm, also developed a strong brewing tradition.

Being a rail center for farm products made St. Paul, and particularly the area south of the city (soon to be the new town of South St. Paul), into one of the nation's major meat packing centers. By the late 1880s, pork packing was St. Paul's most important industry as measured by value of product. Although both Twin Cities had big stockyards, the St. Paul Union Stockyards, founded in 1887, was the most famous. The yards struggled for a number of years due to economic conditions and local competition, but in 1897, Swift and Company, a major force in Chicago meat packing, was lured to open a new plant in South St. Paul on the strength of a 999-year lease. Other major packers soon followed suit, making St. Paul one of the major meat packing centers in the country along with Chicago and Omaha. Local producers also became prominent. The George Hormel Company, founded in Austin in 1891, was the state's largest packer by the 1920s.

Northern Pacific Railway Company train, circa 1875

Other industries, too, grew with time: iron and metallurgical products, boots and shoes, rail car construction and repair, printing and publishing, animal feed, electrical equipment, furniture, butter and dairy products, and woolen goods and textiles. Although processing of the region's wheat crop remained important, the Twin Cities also became a center for processing other crops. By 1900, for example, Minneapolis was the nation's leading market for flax, and was also an important market for rye and barley.

Railroads and the processing of raw materials they brought made vast fortunes for the Twin Cities' new entrepreneurs, making the cities the region's banking center as well as its transport and industrial hub. In 1914 Minneapolis became the home of the Ninth Federal Reserve District on the strength of its banking industry. Minneapolis alone boasted 38 millionaires by 1890.

The new wealth was displayed in stately homes that lined the most fashionable avenues of the two cities. The most notable (and today the best preserved) of these streets is Summit Avenue in St. Paul. There, in 1891, on a crest of the avenue overlooking the Mississippi River, James J. Hill built his mansion. At the time, it was the largest and most elaborate home in the state. Its final price of almost $1 million dollars came with five floors, 13 bathrooms, 22 fireplaces, 16 crystal chandeliers, a two-story sky-lit art gallery, and a 100-foot reception hall. Hill also added what at the time were cutting-edge technologies: central heat, both gas and electric lighting, ventilation, indoor plumbing, security, and communications.

EVERYDAY LIFE

While a few, like Hill, benefited greatly, the new wealth also provided jobs for immigrants and migrants from around the U.S. and around the world. Newcomers flooded into the Twin Cities. Many of these groups formed compact ethnic neighborhoods, with names like Frogtown, Swede Hollow, Bohemian Flats, or "Nordeast." These neighborhoods gave the two cities their character, color, sounds, and smells. One resident remembered walking through Minneapolis's Jewish neighborhood with the director of their local Jewish school: "...as we were going up and down the streets, we could literally smell the Sabbath, the fish and the chicken."

There was no single pattern to the life of working people. Most worked in factories or, if they were well connected or lucky, for the city itself. Their homes were modest places, usually one or two stories. Many families, especially immigrants, took in boarders to supplement the family income. Quite a few housed relatives recently arrived in America. Although renting was common, most families aspired to own their own home. This was a crucial investment for working families and one of the major family assets. Ambitious families might build themselves a duplex, live in one half, and rent out the other, using the rental income to pay off the mortgage. Shopkeepers and craftsmen who owned their own places of business usually lived on the premises with their families. Although there were open plots of land in many neighborhoods until well after the turn of the century, those areas that were used were used intensively. Some lots contained more than one house. Nearly all had sheds, outhouses, stables, or even chicken coops. For those families who had migrated or immigrated from rural areas, keeping some livestock seemed perfectly natural even if city authorities and progressive reformers frowned on the sanitary impact. Most families also kept extensive gardens, especially to grow the vegetables they had known from their homelands which were unavailable in Minnesota. In this way, immigrants introduced such "exotic" fare as tomatoes and zucchini to the local cuisine.

Homes, saloons, ethnic and fraternal halls, and churches and synagogues were the social centers for the working people of the Twin Cities. Although the situation differed in each family and among different cultures, the homes were usually ruled by women, especially in working-class families. It was here that the hard work of culture took place. Immigrant women, largely without the support of mothers and grandmothers left behind in the old country, forged hybrid cultures and customs using old traditions and new ingredients. In addition, many women managed the finances of the family by taking in the paychecks from family members who worked and carefully administering the limited funds, with husbands often kept on a weekly allowance.

Most industrial laborers worked five and a half or six days a week, with ten-hour days and no overtime. Mill workers often came home coated with flour dust, getting in their eyes, mouths, and lungs and causing a wide variety of ailments. Workers returning from a shift in the flour mills "looked like ghosts," one person remembered. Those working in the stockyards and packing houses had it even worse. Working with sharp implements in unsanitary conditions, these workers suffered high rates of accidents and injury in an age when there were few health and safety regulations. Injured workers were often doomed to a life as a recipient of charity if their injuries were serious.

Under these conditions, Minnesota workers began to organize themselves into labor unions. Minnesota's Iron Range had the most significant and thorough organizing activity and it was there that radical groups such as the Socialists, Communists, and International Workers of the World (or "Wobblies") were the most prominent. Nevertheless, most laborers rejected class warfare and the extreme solutions these groups represented. Instead, they sought to be treated with dignity and fairness and to receive wages that would allow them and their families to live without the constant shadow of insecurity and poverty. Union organizing occurred in fits and spurts, often retarded by hostile employers and politicians. St. Paul, with its strong Democratic traditions, tended to be more favorable to labor. The sharpest conflicts occurred in Minneapolis, with the 1934 Teamsters' strike being the most violent incident.

INFRASTRUCTURE

The rate of urban growth reflected the influx of wealth that built the homes on Summit Avenue in St. Paul and Park Avenue in Minneapolis, and which also brought so many working people to the Twin Cities. By 1880 Minneapolis had overtaken St. Paul in size with 46,000 people to the capital city's 41,000. By the turn of the century, St. Paul had 163,000 inhabitants and Minneapolis 202,000.

From their origins along the river banks, both cities expanded, with residences following the development of commerce and industry. An efficient system of street cars in both cities tied the different neighborhoods together by the 1880s. The first lines were proposed in the 1870s and by the

1880s, horse-drawn cars were common. Electric street cars were introduced in 1889, and horse-drawn cars were phased out in a few short years. In 1891 the Minneapolis and St. Paul street cars companies merged into the Twin City Rapid Transit Company, creating a unified urban system. As most streets were unpaved, the cars were often dirty and drivers were required to wash their own. In the winter, the cars could be frigid. Nevertheless, streetcars provided cheap and efficient transportation, and by the 1920s over 500 miles of urban track had been laid for over 1,000 cars, which were usually painted a cheery yellow color.

The streetcar system allowed workers and business-people to get to work and helped establish the custom of separating residences from places of business, allowing industrial and commercial development, and the noise and pollution that went with them, to be kept in discrete areas. Development followed the rails. The street cars also had lines to local lakes, such as White Bear Lake or Lake Minnetonka, which often connected with seasonal excursion boats. In this way families could escape the city for a summer afternoon of swimming, picnicking, or relaxing by the lake.

Until the 1920s, the cities remained relatively compact around a central core. What are today inner-ring suburban communities were still largely rural, with numerous farms that grew produce for the city's tables and markets. In the 1920s, with a booming economy, more automobiles, and better roads, wealthy residents began more and more to move out of the central areas of the cities and build homes close to some of the large lakes.

Yet flight to the suburbs was still many decades away, and the public optimism so characteristic of the Progressive Era was very much in evidence. Nowhere was this more true than in the building of infrastructure. In an age that identified technology and science with progress and progress with goodness and morality, it was only natural that public amenities were a hallmark of a successful city. For the state's two leading cities, often in fierce competition with each other, it was especially important to keep up with the neighbors.

Both cities had installed sewer and water systems by the 1870s, but this fact is slightly misleading. In 1880 St. Paul had 325 miles of streets. It had 24 miles of water

White Bear Lake

mains. In a city of 41,000, only 1,850 households and businesses had city water. Minneapolis had 200 miles of streets and slightly less that 19 miles of water mains. It had just over two miles of sewer. Like most cities the world over, water works and sewer systems were developed quite early in the history of Minnesota's cities and were a point of civic pride, but their reach only extended to a few districts, usually to businesses and wealthy residential areas. Of course, having city water was no guarantee of having good water, since it was mostly drawn from local lakes, rivers, or from wells near those bodies of water. There was no filtration system and it was not unknown to turn on the tap and find small fish in the water.

For the majority of Minnesota's urban residents in cities large and small, life was extremely unsanitary by present-day standards. In addition to the growing human population, each city was home to huge numbers of horses and other livestock. Waste was either buried in shallow pits, in lined vaults, or thrown directly into the nearest body of water. The city of Minneapolis' health officer, Dr. A. H. Salisbury, reported in 1880 to the city council:

> The water from seven wells was analyzed… the analysis showed that five of the wells were absolutely unfit for use…. The well water [in Minneapolis] is generally impure, unwholesome, poisonous, and is becoming more so every year…. We have buried in our light porous soils all manner of filth…. Is it any wonder then that the water has become contaminated?…
>
> The old inhabitants who knew the place in its primitive purity can hardly realize that it is no longer a sanitarium. They call it slander when told that their beloved city is no longer possessed of pure air, pure water, and pure earth, and is in danger of becoming an unhealthy city…. Last year I caused an inspection of some houses where death had occurred to be made. The tabulated results go far to prove that these, which cause almost one-third of our total mortality, are the result of impure air and water, and are therefore preventable. I feel positively sure that were the water from a few miles up the river distributed throughout the city, and every well filled up or pulled up, the use of cesspools and vaults prohibited, and sewers constructed where needed, the death rate… would be reduced to 1 per

1,000 inhabitants, or even less. This would have saved during the last year 182 lives, or, at the usual computation, of a life at $1,000, $182,000.

Not all city officials were willing to deal with the problem. Minneapolis' mayor reported to the U.S. Census Bureau that street cleaning in his city was "well done," but the city health report had a less favorable conclusion:

> The [health] department having no means under its own control of cleaning alleys, gutters, etc., had to depend upon the oftentimes slow movements of the street commissioners.... Under the present plan the health department is held responsible for the sanitary condition of the streets, and yet has no means of keeping them in order, except to request the street commissioners, and then patiently await their slow pleasure.... I discover that it has not been the custom to remove these substances [i.e., refuse matter] from the city limits, at least only such portions as the farmers removed to be used as fertilizers. The scavengers [private waste collectors] and others employed in this business were in the habit of dumping their savory loads in any secluded spot they could find. Hoag's lake was being rapidly filled up with a most abominable variety of filth. I peremptorily discontinued the use of this vicinity as the city dumping ground.

Cities and towns had faced these problems from time immemorial, but what was different about the late nineteenth century was that the leaders of cities like Minneapolis and St. Paul were determined to change the living conditions of its citizens forever. Armed with new, though imperfectly understood information on the link between filth and disease and possessed of the reforming spirit of the Progressive Era, health officials, doctors, social workers, politicians, and civic activists began a great campaign to "clean up" their cities. Yet for progressive Minnesotans, this also meant far more than neater streets, for it also implied moral and even racial hygiene. In 1915 this ideology was summed up in a report on the development of parks in St. Paul. Park official Cyrus P. Stimson wrote:

The central problems of civilization have to do with the conservation of the race itself—the breeding, nurture and maturing of successive generations capable of survival in the confraternity of nations—the conservation of precisely those human qualities and values without which race survival unto a conquering civilization are impossible. The application of known principals of social science, in the prevention of human waste and inefficiency, at the roots of causation, is now recognized as a legitimate function of governments.

Urban Minnesota's effort to clean up started with a raft of new laws and civic regulations put in place by local governments. Though often maligned, city governments in this era proved an effective tool for social reformers. In 1883, St. Paul issued its first comprehensive Health Ordinances, including:

Sec. 74. No owner or possessor of any animal which shall have died, shall suffer the same to lie on any public ground, street, lane, alley, or any private lot or place within the city; nor shall any person throw or leave any such animal, or any vegetables or decayed animal matter, or any slops or filth whatever, solid or fluid, into any pool of water in said city.

Must-See Sites: Lindbergh House, Little Falls

Dedicated to the life and accomplishments of one of America's great aviators, the Lindbergh Home tells the full scope of Lindbergh's life, beginning with his boyhood along the Mississippi in Little Falls, Minnesota. It contains the original family furnishings and possessions, and hundreds of photos and artifacts in an expanded visitor center. Visitors can also step inside a full-scale replica of the Spirit of St. Louis cockpit and see hundreds of photographs and artifacts, many of them never before publicly displayed.

Contact: (320) 632-3154; E-mail: lindbergh@mnhs.org; Web: www.mnhs.org

Location: Charles Lindbergh House, 1620 Lindbergh Drive, S. Little Falls.

By the turn of the century, both Minneapolis and St. Paul as well as many smaller communities) were making substantial annual investments in expanding and improving local infrastructure, particularly water, sewer, and lights. In 1882, St. Paul purchased its water works from the private company that had previously operated them, symbolizing the new trust being placed in government to reform and improve life. By 1901, although still far from complete, sewer mileage in St. Paul increased to almost half the mileage of streets, growing from less than 10 percent twenty years before. By the 1930s, 93 percent of all Twin Cities residents had indoor toilets, 78 percent had both hot and cold running water, and another 21 percent had at least cold running water in their homes. This resulted in a great transformation in the way people lived: They were cleaner and healthier and had more leisure time.

Street paving began in earnest in the 1880s, though many roads remained unpaved into the 1920s. A major effort had to be made to keep streets clean. In St. Paul, streets in "important residence districts" such as Summit Avenue had a regular person assigned to clean them every day. Most paved streets were swept once a week, some every day. One city report noted: "As early as possible in spring and as soon as the streets are practically free of ice and snow, a large gang of street cleaners is put to work scraping and picking the paving streets, ridding them of the winter's accumulation of dirt and rubbish." St. Paul employed about 15 men full time as street sweepers: "The men are all neatly uniformed and provided with push carts, shovel and broom, and are employed during the entire season."

Each city instituted regulations designed to prevent the spread of disease, including the use of "pest houses," where people with infectious diseases were quarantined. In an era when only the very ill or the well-to-do saw a doctor on a regular basis, the earliest hospitals in the Twin Cities were founded by religious institutions. Home remedies, herbal infusions, and, in many immigrant communities, the use of traditional healers and midwives prevailed. St. Paul's first hospital, St. Joseph's, was founded in 1853 by the Catholic archdiocese. City and County Hospital, a public institution, was founded in 1873. In Minneapolis, the Episcopalian church founded St. Barnabas Hospital in 1871. Northwestern

Hospital (later Abbott-Northwestern) opened in 1882. That same year, the University of Minnesota gave a major boost to the status of health care in the two cities when it established its own medical and dental school. A separate university hospital began in 1905. By 1910 St. Paul alone boasted about 250 doctors and assorted homeopaths as well as 150 dentists.

During the Progressive Era (1880-1920) which idealized positivism and social reform, health care was increasingly democratized and more information reached the public. Some of this information was misleading and even fraudulent, as quacks tried to take advantage of a growing public concern. Private charitable associations, however, became a growing force in public health. One example was the Minneapolis Visiting Nurses Association, founded in 1902. Funded mainly with private donations, these nurses visited homes where doctors were unavailable or unaffordable. They placed a particular emphasis on the health needs of women and children. In 1908 the association established a camp at Glenwood Park for children stricken with tuberculosis. The nurses also worked to displace traditional midwives. As one nurse, Hildegarde Ostrom, put it in 1923: "One great difficulty in our maternity work then was that most of our foreign mothers refused the care of physicians and engaged ignorant midwives."

Public health soon became a source of pride and civic rivalry. In 1910, when St. Paul received a prize from the Paris Exhibition as the world's healthiest city and when its recorded death rate was claimed to be substantially lower than neighboring Minneapolis, city leaders were quick to point out the advantages of living in "salubrious St. Paul."

With public health and cleanliness came moral uplift. According to the language of the time, the "shiftless" were put to work, and the "inferior" immigrants from eastern and southern Europe were instructed on how to act as much like their "superior" northern and western European counterparts as possible. Many institutions took a less condescending approach, and, although burdened with the prejudices of the era, most reformers sought to do good. Organizations such as the Young Men's Christian Association (YMCA), the Boy Scouts, the Salvation Army, and a wide range of other charitable institutions tried to be both teachers of practical skills and moral tutors. Settlement

The city is building up so rapidly that all unoccupied intervals within its limits are being cut down to the very boundaries of the building lots... An open, ample breathing space for all the people is already hard to find.... As it is, where could we hold a Fourth of July celebration or hear an evening concert from instruments requiring vast space for their finest efforts?... Public parks have come to be recognized as institutions essential to the health, as well as the happiness, of thickly settled communities. Children suffer from the privations, pine and sicken, and fill untimely graves because [they are] cut off from a healthful provision of God's light and the pure atmosphere that circulates among the trees and through broad, vast expanses.

It was not until 1883 that city voters in Minneapolis passed a referendum approving the creation of city parks.

Led by Charles Loring and later Theodore Wirth in Minneapolis and by Joseph Wheelock in St. Paul (all of whom gave their names to local parks or parkways), both cities threw themselves into park building with a will. In Minneapolis, Loring Park (then Central Park) was established in 1883. The major local lakes became ideal park venues, although their present state has been much modified through drainage of nearby wetlands and dredging and deepening. Lake Harriet was developed between 1883 and 1898, and Lake Calhoun between 1886 and 1909. Lake of Isles parkland was acquired in 1903 and Lake Nokomis in 1907. In 1911 park development reached a high point of civic ambition as Minneapolis' western lakes were linked together with a channel that allowed pleasure boats to pass from one to the other. (Lakes in poorer districts of the city were not so lucky. Lake Sandy in working-class and largely eastern European Northeast Minneapolis was gradually filled in with sediment dredged from Lake of the Isles.) By 1912 Minneapolis had 3,689 acres of parks, including 27 parks larger than five acres, 40 smaller parks and triangles, and 12 public playgrounds.

St. Paul, too, developed impressive park systems. Early parks, which pre-dated those in Minneapolis by a few years, were small urban squares of green space. Yet in 1887 St. Paul founded Como Park around Lake Como. Like many parks of its day, early Como Park was meant as a quasi-

Lake Harriet at sunset

natural refuge from urban life. Filled with trees, curving walkways (unlike the straight grid-like streets), ponds, and gardens, the park was meant to be a quiet escape from the hustle of city life. There were spaces for public band concerts and similar cultural activities. In the 1920s and 1930s, Como Park was gradually redeveloped to emphasize planned activities such as golf and baseball. St. Paul also acquired land around Lake Phalen after the turn of the century that began Phalen Park. By 1915 the city had over 1,400 acres of parks, aside from boulevards and playgrounds. Following the bicycle craze of the 1890s, St. Paul also developed extensive bike trails. By 1901, there were 50 miles of bicycle paths in the city and over 32 miles more just beyond the city limits.

The Twin Cities were not alone in developing large park systems. Minnesota's "third city," Duluth, developed a system that rivaled its two larger Minnesota sisters. Much of Duluth's park development occurred in the 1920s under the direction of Mayor Samuel Snively. During his first administration in the early 1920s, park space in Duluth tripled as the city worked to complete what would become Skyline Parkway, a system of scenic roads, parks, and overlooks that snaked for 25 miles along the ridgeline above the city and provided panoramic views of the harbor and Lake Superior. In 1932 the city had one acre of park for every 41 residents, the highest proportion of any city in the United States. (One acre per 100 inhabitants was considered impressive.) Much of the construction of this park was completed with private donations of land or money, including by the mayor himself.

URBAN RIVALRY

Minnesota's major cities developed their characters during this era and also created many of their enduring traditions. Many of these revolved around public entertainments that found a venue in the state's newly created parks and public spaces. One of the best known and most unique has the practice of winter frolics. Although several Minnesota cities created such events, the best known and most enduring has been the St. Paul Winter Carnival. Overcoming concerns that such a festival would cement the state's reputation as the nation's icebox, local leaders and promoters launched the tradition in the winter of 1885–86. The Winter Carnival featured winter sports (especially sledding, skating, snowshoeing, and skiing), ice sculptures, and an elaborate mock battle in which the forces of fire and heat are supposed to overcome those of ice and cold. Yet the most remembered aspect of the carnivals was always the huge ice castles. The ice castle became the trademark of the Winter Carnival and a symbol of the city's ability to turn what would otherwise be a liability into an asset.

Despite being side by side, Minneapolis and St. Paul developed very different characters and maintain this distinctiveness to the present day. St. Paul was shaped by its close association with state government and with the Catholic Church. As the seat of government, St. Paul was always able to maintain a certain parity with its larger and more prosperous rival to the west by being more keenly political. The Saintly City was the seat of the state's Catholic Archdiocese and a locus for Irish-American political power. (Its bishops and archbishops have always been Irish Americans.) Although the total number of Irish in St. Paul was never especially large, they were able to build political coalitions with many other groups. A crucial factor in their success was the fact that James J. Hill's wife, Mary, came from a strong Irish Catholic working-class background. (Hill himself was born a Protestant and personally seems to have been areligious.) Her position as the first lady of the city's social scene (a role that was not of her choosing), helped integrate Irish Americans into the city's leadership far more quickly than in many other cities. James Hill also built ties to the powerful archbishop, John Ireland. Ireland helped Hill bring Catholic immigrants to settle Hill's railroad lands and Hill made a very public gift of land on the highest point in the city to build a new Cathedral, completed in 1912.

St. Paul developed much like an overgrown small town. It had strong blue-collar neighborhoods that usually voted Democratic, and it was compact and familiar. People knew each other by sight. What it lacked in economic growth and high culture, it made up for in tradition and a kind of understated elegance.

Minneapolis was defined by growth. It was a city of businessmen and Progressives. In Minneapolis, Scandinavian

Wets vs. Drys

Minnesota's relationship with liquor has been a stormy one. Among the state's earliest American settlers, the battle over illegal liquor—and its sale to Native Americans—provoked sharp divisions. The first wave of settlers from the east were mostly Yankees who brought a strong puritanical tradition that saw "demon rum" as the work of the devil. On the other hand, the many immigrants from central and eastern Europe and especially the large German community, made Minnesota an early center for brewing. German settlers opened beer gardens and saloons and celebrated Octoberfest as in the old country. The division over alcohol also had strong religious overtones. Alcohol's opponents (called drys) tended to be Protestant and were often aligned with those who favored restrictions on immigration. Supporters (called wets) were heavily Catholic and immigrant. (Of course, there were many exceptions to this rule and Catholic teetotalers and Protestant wets were not unknown.)

The struggle was cast as a moral issue in which reformers sought to better society through eliminating social ills, and alcohol was viewed as root of many social ills. Groups such as the Women's Christian Temperance Union (WCTU) fused religious idealism with the progressive rhetoric of social reform and women's activism. By the 1890s, WCTU chapters had spread across the state of Minnesota. WCTU was a bastion of English-speaking Protestant women who were assuming a visible public role for the first time in their lives as guardians of the moral order. They enlisted their husbands, sons, and brothers, who were often community leaders, in the cause of prohibition.

Local WCTU chapters pursued a two-fold strategy. First, they used local newspapers to spread their message, often through the use of heart-wrenching stories of family tragedy. The stories followed a particular formula, featuring a drunken husband whose alcoholism threatens to destroy the family, a long-suffering, good-hearted wife who seeks in vain to keep her man from the bottle, and pathetic, ragged, half-starved children who say things like "Daddy, please don't beat Mommy on Christmas Eve!" The fact that there were actually some families like this in most communities added verisimilitude.

The second part of the strategy was to push for local bans on the sale and consumption of liquor. Since many small towns derived significant income from saloon licenses, this move created political complications. Moves toward prohibition were opposed by a loose coalition of saloon owners, Catholics, and those who bridled at moral lectures on "demon rum." Referenda on local options were heated and often split communities squarely down the middle. Some Minnesota towns went dry for a few years until anti-prohibition forces staged a comeback. The saloons would reopen for a while until the drys regrouped and made a comeback.

Towns that went dry usually found their measures to be totally ineffective. Drinkers simply traveled to nearby towns and stocked up, while local saloons sold illegal liquor under the table. Elected town marshals were often reluctant to intervene for fear of being voted out of office by one side or the other. When the town of Marshall went dry in 1901, the effort proved a failure. The local pro-temperance editor bemoaned the fact that his city was

> a no-license town, with many blind pigs,
> much boot-legging, considerable wholesale
> shipping-in, and lots of drunkenness and
> disorder, and no municipal control of the
> traffic in booze. While Marshall was 'dry' there
> was not a Saturday night, and few other nights
> of week, when the express wagons did not come
> from the depots loaded with beer kegs and cases
> and demijohns and jugs, to say nothing of wide
> open violations along the street.

Such local fiascos may have inspired Minnesota Congressman Andrew Volstead to author the National Prohibition Act, which passed Congress in 1919. Yet this measure, too, failed to curb alcohol. Minnesota, with its long and unpoliced northern border, became a prime shipping point for Canadian liquor heading south. Minnesota entrepreneurs large and small also got in on the act, producing their own homemade hooch. Central Minnesota had its "Minnesota 13," a whiskey produced from number 13 variety corn that was allegedly better than anything made before Prohibition. Local and national gangsters set up their own distilling or importing operations in the state, using cities like St. Paul as outposts in their illegal empire.

The end of Prohibition did not stop the move to restrict alcohol, and some local communities remained more or less dry well into the late twentieth century. In some towns, restaurants served only 3.2 beer. Other restaurants had "bottle clubs" where patrons could store their own personal liquor while the restaurants served only the drink mixes. Another side effect of the state's long battle over alcohol was the creation of municipal liquor stores in many towns. At the end of Prohibition, communities with a strong "dry" tradition often opted to open such stores as a way to carefully regulate "off sale" liquor.

Yet the state's tradition of regulating vice did not end with alcohol. Since the 1970s, Minnesota has been one of the states most aggressive in restricting and banning public smoking, an echo of earlier days when "wets" and "drys" battled it out on the editorial pages and at the ballot box.

Despite such scandals, politics in the two cities, and indeed in Minnesota as a whole, has always had a reputation for being honest. Although it has often been mythologized, the reputation is not altogether unfounded. No major electoral scandals mar Minnesota's history (at least since statehood). Yet its political life has not been as staid as might first appear.

From statehood to about 1890, Republicans dominated most major federal and statewide offices. They drew their support from Yankees as well as the growing Norwegian and Swedish communities. Germans were divided— strongly supporting the legacy of Lincoln but increasingly troubled by the Republicans' growing image as the party that opposed immigration and liquor. Irish, Poles, and Jews, by contrast, tended to vote Democratic. Early state governors were almost all Old Stock Americans. The first non-Yankee governor, the Norwegian immigrant Knute Nelson, did not gain office until 1892.

Toward the end of the 1880s, however, rural areas of the Midwest and Minnesota especially were growing increasingly restive. In particular, there was growing resentment at the economic and political domination that railroads and major processors in the Twin Cities seemed to be exercising over the lives and fortunes of farmers in the vast midwestern hinterland. The first major post-Civil War farm protest movement, the Grange, had known brief success in the 1870s, but in Minnesota many rural areas of the state were still in the process of settlement. The formation of the Farmer's Alliance had a much greater impact on Minnesota politics, producing for the first time a legislature dominated by a different party from that of the governor.

From the 1890s, a series of third parties challenged the Republicans and Democrats for leadership in Minnesota. These Populists and Progressives found their most able local spokesman in Ignatius Donnelly, who proved a brilliant public speaker, though a less successful candidate. In many ways this movement cut most deeply into the support of the Democrats, whose gubernatorial candidate in 1920, for example, got only 10 percent of the vote. Pragmatic Republican leaders, like Nelson, tried to enact measures to mollify angry farmers. At the same time, growing socialist, communist, and radical movements among Scandinavians (especially Finns) added to the complicated mix and raised the possibility of an alliance between farmers and industrial workers.

The most significant third party movement in Minnesota began just before the U.S. entry into World War I. The Non-Partisan League was founded in North Dakota by farmers opposed to the power of St. Paul railroads. It quickly spread to Minnesota as well. Among its goals were lower farm taxes; state ownership of packing and processing plants, grain elevators, and warehouses; state insurance for hail protection, and life, accident, and old-age insurance; an eight-hour day for all workers save farmers; and a progressive income tax. In 1920, drawing support from Minnesotans disenchanted with the strongly pro-intervention, anti-immigrant stance of state government during World War I, as well as from those hurt by the post-war recession, the NPL made an especially strong showing in the governors' race. The NPL candidate, Charles Lindbergh, Sr. (the father of the soon-to-be famous aviator), won one-third of all votes and came in second. Yet the Republicans managed to maintain a plurality in most major elections, since their opposition was essentially split in two. Disenchantment among industrial workers with a lack of support from Minnesota Democrats led to the formation of the Minnesota Farmer–Labor Party, a fusion of NPL supporters, union members, and various socialist elements.

The onset of the Depression allowed the party to score its greatest success with the 1930 election of Floyd B. Olsen as governor. In national races, the Farmer-Laborites supported Franklin D. Roosevelt and the policies of the New Deal, and Olsen was more than happy for Minnesota to receive its share of federal dollars to employ out-of-work Minnesotans. Yet Olsen's election proved the high-water mark for the party. There was no clear successor to the charismatic Olsen—sometimes called Minnesota's FDR—and splits soon appeared in the party. This came to the fore in 1938 as a growing rift emerged between moderates and more radical socialist and communist sympathizers. In that year, the Democrats regained much lost ground. The communist–Nazi alliance in Europe in 1939 only furthered divisions within the party's left wing and in 1944 the Farmer–Labor party merged with the Democrats to form the Democratic Farmer–Labor (DFL) party. This ended a major era of third-party activity in the state and the idea would remain dormant for many decades thereafter.

In politics, as in economics and culture, the Twin Cities were the locus of urban life in the Upper Midwest. Yet there were many other small cities that developed a significant standing, though always in the shadows of Minneapolis and St. Paul. One of these cities was Rochester. Founded by Yankees, Rochester was a local trade center like many other communities in the region. It grew to be something more, thanks to the fame of the Mayo Clinic. In the late 1880s and 1890s, two brothers, Drs. William and Charles Mayo, joined forces with an order of Catholic nuns, the Sisters of St. Francis, to form one of the world's best-known medical establishments. The Mayos pioneered the use of sterilization techniques developed by Dr. Joseph Lister as well as the practice of maintaining detailed patient histories. The success rate of their treatments, which exceeded most other hospitals and clinics of the day, gained local, national, and eventually international attention. As the number of patients coming to Rochester increased, so did the specialization and number of hospitals and doctors. Presidents, royalty, and celebrities of all sorts, as well as ordinary folk, came to be cured and put the city of Rochester on the map, making it economically and culturally distinctive.

Another city with a special character was Duluth, Minnesota's third-largest city. The city was built by iron ore and timber. In 1890, its population stood at 33,000. A decade later, as the mining boom in northern Minnesota kicked in, its population was nearly 53,000, an increase of almost two thirds. By 1920 it had grown to about 100,000. Duluth became a transshipment and processing point for the raw materials extracted from northern Minnesota's mines and forests. With the opening of the St. Lawrence Seaway in the 1950s, it became an international port, the furthest inland of any such port. Although the city's development gave it a strongly blue-collar flavor, during Duluth's heyday, the wealth created by northern Minnesota's new industries stayed in the city. The wealthy built their mansions along the shores of the great lake. The city's wealth then allowed it to maintain a cultural life and aspirations somewhat above those of most medium-

Famous Minnesotans:
Charles M. Schulz

Born Nov. 26, 1922, Minneapolis.
Died Feb. 12, 2000, Santa Rosa, Calif.

Possibly the most famous cartoonist ever, Charles Monroe Schulz was the son of a German immigrant barber in Minneapolis. The family lived in St. Paul for most of Schulz's childhood, during which time they acquired a black and white dog, Spike, who later became the inspiration for the cartoon character Snoopy. The young Schulz showed an early talent for drawing and had his first drawing published at the age of 15. Later Schulz took a few college art courses and served as combat soldier in the U.S. Army in Europe during World War II. In 1947 he began a weekly cartoon strip in the St. Paul Pioneer Press called "Li'l Folks." In 1950 he signed a contract with United Features Syndicate for a strip based on "Li'l Folks," called "Peanuts." By 1952 the strip was featured in over 40 newspapers nationwide. The cartoon's popularity skyrocketed. Dozens of anthologies were published, and the strip was used to illustrate everything from the Bible to the U.S. space program. Television specials, beginning with "A Charlie Brown Christmas," began in 1966 and the musical "You're a Good Man, Charlie Brown" became the most frequently performed musical in American theatrical history. Schulz won virtually every cartoonist award in existence, as well as special awards from numerous governments, organizations, and universities. By 1984 "Peanuts" was in 2,000 newspapers worldwide and reached over 100 million people daily. Schulz retired from cartooning in January 2000 after 50 years. His last cartoon appeared on the day after he died, and "Peanuts" remains the most popular cartoon strip ever.

sized industrial cities. Such aspirations were aided by the creation of a branch of the University of Minnesota in Duluth in 1902, which began as a school for teachers and later evolved into a full-fledged university. But the early iron boom that made Duluth ended by the 1920s and the city struggled to maintain itself, showing virtually no population gain for decades thereafter.

World War I proved a watershed for Minnesota, both urban and rural, in that it marked the beginning of a long series of migrations out of the countryside and into the cities. The war itself called some 126,000 Minnesotans to stand to the colors, and these service people came back having seen more of the world. Although Progressivism lived on after the war, faith in human progress had been seriously shaken by the horrors of the war. One of the last attempts of this era to reform moral behavior was Prohibition, the legislation for which was written by Andrew Volstead, a congressman from Granite Falls in western Minnesota.

The 1920s had a particularly important effect on the Twin Cities as they became ever more closely tied to the national mass culture through movies, traveling jazz musicians, mass circulation magazines, and professional sports. The cities in turn re-exported this new culture to its own rural and small-town hinterland. The Twin Cities also became notorious during that era as a haven for criminals and bootleggers. Both cities developed an active underworld. In Minneapolis, Isidore "Kid Can" Blumenfeld held sway until the 1950s. Yet it was St. Paul that became known as the gangsters' resort. Local mobsters and the city police developed "the O'Connor System," named after sometime St. Paul Police Chief John O'Connor. Criminals paid off the police on arrival and agreed to commit no crimes. In return, the police left them alone and even at times tipped them off to impending federal raids. During the 1920s, St. Paul hosted such notorious figures as John Dillinger, Alvin Karpis, and Ma Barker and her boys. Local residents got a guilty thrill by rubbing shoulders with "Public Enemies" at the city's many popular nightclubs and dancehalls as jazz played and illegal liquor flowed. In the early 1930s, with the end of Prohibition and its profits, the system began to break down, and O'Connor, who then headed the anti-kidnapping squad, actually worked with gangsters to identify wealthy St. Paulites to kidnap for ransom. This led to the Barker-Karpis gang's kidnappings of brewer William Hamm and banker Edward Bremer, crimes for which they and O'Connor were eventually caught.

The Depression ended the high times of the 1920s and wrecked the fortunes of many Twin Cities businessmen, including the builder of the Foshay Tower. Yet the hard economic times did not slow the influx of new residents, and both cities, particularly Minneapolis, continued to grow in population as people left farms and small towns. The tensions of the era were not absent either. In July 1934, striking Teamsters clashed with Minneapolis police in the state's bloodiest labor dispute. Two strikers were killed and dozens wounded in the "Bloody Friday" massacre.

The coming of World War II to America in 1941 effectively ended the Depression and, like other major urban areas, the two cities geared up for war production as over 300,000 Minnesotans joined the armed forces. In addition to producing food, local companies such as Honeywell produced weapons and material for the Allied cause in massive quantities, greatly increasing output and expanding the demand for labor. Local women and older, retired male workers poured into the workforce and more came from the farms and small towns to make up the shortfall in labor.

Already by the end of 1944, many Minnesota cities faced a housing crunch and some instituted emergency housing plans to create short-term housing for returning servicemen and their families. The booming economy fueled a period of phenomenal growth that continued after the war and into the 1960s. This growth raised wages and allowed more families to purchase larger homes. Although some suburbanization occurred prior to the war, it was this post-war era that began suburbanization in earnest. Areas that had once been rural or semi-rural were gradually filled in with new houses, houses that seemed to spring up almost overnight. New cities, such as Roseville, St. Louis Park, Brooklyn Park, Fridley, Bloomington, and Richfield, came to life and the core cities themselves expanded. Although population in the Twin Cities metropolitan area had always

Sailboats on Lake Nokomis

Must-See Sites:
Voyageurs National Park

The park, established in 1975, lies in the southern part of the Canadian Shield, representing some of the oldest exposed rock formations in the world. This bedrock has been shaped and carved by at least four periods of glaciation. The topography of the park is rugged and varied; rolling hills are interspersed between bogs, beaver ponds, swamps, islands, small lakes, and four large lakes. In the years since the last glaciation, a thin layer of soil has been created that supports the boreal forest ecosystem, the "North Woods" of Voyageurs National Park. This land is rich in human history and was named for the voyageurs, French Canadian canoe-men who traveled these waters in their birch-bark canoes from the Great Lakes to the interior of the western United States and Canada. Modern voyageurs continue to ply these waters. The water, accompanying scenery, geology, and rich cultural and natural resources giving Voyageurs its national significance, merits its protection for the enjoyment of present and future generations. On the northern edge of Minnesota's border, 55 miles of the park meander along the Canadian border with Ontario. Voyageurs is a water-based park. Access to the Kabetogama peninsula, the islands, and nearly all of the park's shoreline is by watercraft. Free public boat ramps and parking are available at the park's visitor centers and at the Kabetogama State Forest Campgrounds.

Contact: Headquarters (218) 283-9821; Rainy Lake Visitor Center (218) 286-5258 TTY (218) 286-5261; Kabetogama Lake Visitor Center (218) 875-2111; Ash River Visitor Center (218) 374-3221; Web: www.nps.gov/voya/

Location: Voyageurs is about 15 miles east of International Falls and 300 miles north of Minneapolis-St. Paul.

grown, this new growth was less obvious in terms of the overall number of new inhabitants than in the expanding area of settlement. Small houses on small lots that were the norm in so many blue-collar neighbors became less popular and were supplanted by larger lots and larger houses with more lawns. Lawns, once a symbol of wealth and leisure, became the norm for the middle class. As the second half of the century dawned, Minnesota's urban region was set to grow in size as never before.

8

The Long Afternoon of Outstate Minnesota

Throughout most of its history Minnesota has been a rural state, its character and self-image defined by farms, mines, small towns, forests, and the lake country. Like the urban centers of the state, Minnesota beyond the Twin Cities—sometimes called outstate Minnesota, or, euphemistically, Greater Minnesota—has never been static or homogeneous. It has undergone so many changes since the time of settlement that few of its residents today, let alone those who live in the urban centers, remember what the area was like. So it is subject to various stereotypes dreamed up by urbanized interpreters, being either a quaint and somewhat offbeat Lake Wobegeon of Garrison Keillor fame, where people speak a dialect heavily laced with Norwegian accents, or the dark and culturally barren Main Street of Sinclair Lewis.

The reality is far more complicated and interesting.

At the time of statehood, rural inhabitants outnumbered urban Minnesotans by about ten to one. The migration of settlers into the rural areas of the state continued to be very high until about 1890, when the number began to level off. At the same time, Minnesota's urban population continued to grow dramatically. By about 1930, the two sectors of the state reached equilibrium. (This was a decade after the urban population in the nation as a whole exceeded that of the nation's rural population.) Although large farm families helped the state's rural population grow, the reality is that in rural Minnesota, growth and decline occurred simultaneously. Even during its boom years of pioneer settlement, rural Minnesota suffered out-migration.

MYTH AND REALITY

There was never any one single rural Minnesota, but many. Economically, the Iron Range, with its heavy concentration of wage labor, in some ways resembled urban Minnesota more than the farming regions. Areas in the lake country of north-central Minnesota developed a mixed agricultural and resort economy. Even the purely agricultural areas were very different from one another. In the cut over areas left behind by the loggers, farmers scratched a hard living from the thin soil. In the south, the corn and hog-feeding operations that characterized the Corn Belt came to predominate by World War II. In the Red River valley, big bonanza farms imported migrant workers from Mexico to harvest sugar beets, and the flat valley floor proved ideal for wheat. Dairying predominated in the east with smaller, more intensive farms, while grain was king in the west with large farms. Yet for each of these generalizations, there were countless exceptions.

For most of its residents, rural Minnesota was something far more personal. It was a specific place marked by memory, struggles, and victories. Marjorie Myers Douglas, who moved from the city to a farm in western Minnesota with her husband, recalled being at first curious what life on a farm would be like:

> With a year-old daughter in diapers and no running water in the farmhouse, I soon found my curiosity satisfied. I quickly developed a real respect for people who can *do* things! Following their example, I learned how to do things, too—bake bread, stake tomatoes, mother newborn animals, raise three lively children, and teach Sunday school…. Those seventeen years, against the backdrop of hard work and constant worry about the weather, I heard marvelous stories of farm happenings. Other stories were told [to] me: how Marj, armed only with a dull ax, faced eighty five hens and eventually won. And I began to understand how people in this midwestern farm neighborhood lived out the independence and steadfast moral sense so highly valued by Minnesotans.

There was little romance in the reality of farm life. The work was and is hard, even after machinery began to make the job easier. Accident rates for farm work were extremely high. There was little time for vacation and no days off. Children worked along with adults, leading to tension between generations. The idea of staying after school to play sports was not an option for many farm kids well into the 1960s. In extreme cases, parents struggling to make ends meet could turn their children into virtual slaves, causing many of them to leave farming forever at the first opportunity.

Farming has rarely provided a decent living. As standards of living have increased in society as a whole, most farm families could not keep pace, leading to greater pressures on young people to leave rural areas. Periodic "farm crises" of the last 100 years were only the most extreme cases of the recurring struggles caused by the very success of the farmers themselves. More food, produced more and more efficiently, leads to lower and lower prices. Farmers faced with lower prices for their products inevitably try to produce even more to make up the shortfall. To produce more food demands more land machinery, fertilizer, and pesticide, all of which costs money. If farmers borrow money to build bigger farms, they take a major gamble. Any combination of economic recession, bad weather, crop diseases, or a hundred other things could turn the gamble to disaster.

Of course, not all farming traditions were the same. Many Minnesota ethnic groups saw the farm as a stepping stone. Yankee farmers tended to send their children to school or train them for white-collar jobs. Scandinavians and French Canadians remained on the farm longer, but by the second generation, the lure of an easier life in white-collar jobs made itself felt. Scandinavians, with a strong educational tradition, also had the means to educate many rural young people who rarely returned to a life of toil on the land once they had been to college. Germans, and especially German Catholics, as well as Belgians and Dutch, placed a high value on getting and keeping land. Their children and grandchildren became farmers in far greater numbers. As other groups moved on, these farmers bought out their neighbors and left their farms to their children. Thus, many areas where the farm population was ethnically mixed to begin with became more German or more Belgian over time as the children and grandchildren of the immigrants started farms of their own.

In the mines and forests of northern Minnesota, a different kind of rural life existed. As on farms, physical labor took precedence. The state's iron miners had arguably some of the toughest jobs and none were tougher than the deep-shaft miners of the Cuyuna Range. Each day, the miners would descend hundreds of feet into the earth to chisel out the manganese-rich iron ore. It was hard, dangerous work and the chance of being killed or injured was always present. This was made clear in 1924 when the

Autumn corn fields, Lanesboro

Milford mine near Crosby suffered the worst mining disaster in the state's history. Some believe the mine management ran the shafts too close to a nearby lake. Whatever the reason, on February 5, 1924, part of the mine collapsed, sending a flood of water and mud into the shafts. Forty-one men died that day and only seven escaped. Some of the victims were found buried in mud, their arms wrapped around each other.

Such tragedies, however, were not what most iron rangers remember. The small mining towns were places of ethnic diversity and camaraderie born of shared danger. Each community held its own score of saloons, social halls, and churches (and a few synagogues as well).

In the far north, trapping, hunting, and fishing remained economically important well into the twentieth century. Independent commercial fisherman plied the dangerous waters of Lake Superior in small boats until the 1940s when most of them finally left the business.

Although some individual trappers continued to work for many decades, by World War II, overexploitation and competition from commercial fur farms made the business unprofitable. Many individuals and families continued to eke a living out of the wilderness. In 1920, Charles Ira Cook met one large, mixed-race family that trapped together during the winter:

> During the trapping season, the family split up into pairs. One older person always stayed at home with the two youngest children and set traps and snares in the vicinity of the cabin; the others picked their favorite companion and in groups of two struck out on snowshoes, packs on their backs, for a thirty-day period on their assigned trapping grounds. There was a great deal of rivalry to see who could bring in the most fur, and the crowning glory was to beat their father, who teamed up with his favorite, Mike. Jack [the father] supervised the crews and placed the more ambitious and experienced pairs in the territories where the highest-priced fur was to be found. Fisher, martin, otter, mink, and silver fox were the most sought after animals, and the most difficult to outwit. Mrs. Powell and her oldest daughter were the stiffest competition, and more often than not, they brought in the prize catches. Beaver were plentiful, were easy to trap, and brought good prices on the market.... Jack had over a hundred of the most beautiful, carefully selected, fully prime, matched muskrat hides that one could imagine. They had been willow-tanned in Indian fashion by Mrs. Powell and the girls, and were soft as chamois..

For all its romance, however, living in the north woods on a year-round basis was simply not a lifestyle most families could pursue. Increasing standards of living, better education, and the possibility of making more money at wage labor lured more and more young people to the towns and cities.

HICKS VS. SLICKERS

For all outstate Minnesotans, and especially farmers, the lure of the bigger towns was strong, but the relationship was never without its moments of tension. There were "city slickers" and "country hicks." Jokes, usually fairly vulgar, flew back and forth. The "hicks" were portrayed as ignorant rubes, while the "slickers" were effete and prissy. The standard punch line usually involved a farmer going to town or a city person visiting the farm. Sometimes joking turned serious and there were fistfights, especially at dances or anytime unmarried young people congregated.

A more lasting conflict occurred between local merchants, particularly bankers, and farmers. Farmers were generally cash-poor. Their main source of income arrived in the fall after harvest. To get supplies and staple goods at the stores usually meant buying on credit. If a harvest were bad or late, the merchant might not get paid in full. A merchant who thought he was not going to get paid might cut off credit. But that, in turn, might cause his customers to go elsewhere. One small-town merchant in the 1880s ruefully referred to himself as the "cashier of Wilno." Farmers who borrowed from banks could expand their operations, but the farm economy was unforgiving in the long term. Conservative, recently immigrated farm families often distrusted banks and preferred a long-term strategy of slow property acquisition and reliance on family labor and connections.

For all the problems between them, the towns still drew farmers. This became more and more common as the automobile reached the countryside and farm families could travel more easily. There were the usual attractions of shops, saloons, and social activities. There were also special attractions, such as traveling circuses, vaudeville acts, revival-tent preachers, and Chautauquas. Circuses such as the Ringling Brothers toured Minnesota each year. In the

Must-See Sites: James J. Hill House, St. Paul

The quintessential Gilded Age mansion, the Hill House, built in 1891, was the family home of rail baron James J. Hill, builder of the Great Northern Railway. Rugged red sandstone, massive scale, fine detail, and ingenious mechanical systems recall family and servant life in the 1890s, when the home was the premier address of the city's social life. The James J. Hill House is now a multiple-use historic house museum offering guided tours, educational programs, neighborhood tours, lectures, concerts, dramatic programs, and art exhibitions for the general public.

Contact: (651) 297-2555; E-mail: hillhouse@ mnhs.org; Web: www.mnhs.org

Location: One half block west of Cathedral of St. Paul on Summit Avenue, St. Paul.

summer of 1893 small-town residents were stupefied by giant-print advertising in local newspapers that read: "Ringling Bros. World's Greatest Shows! Real Roman Hippodrome… Tremendous Revival of the Circus Maximus… Si Hassan Ben Ali's Troupe of Arabs. Mikado's Troupe of Royal Japanese Equilibrists. Largest Living Giraff. Standing Full 18 Feet in Height… Moscow's Silver Chimes, Golden Steam Calliope." These acts made it seem as if the whole world were coming to each community to perform just for the average farm family and their small-town neighbors. There was historical and cultural pageantry too. In 1899 Buffalo Bill's Wild West Show brought rural Minnesota a "realistic reproduction" of the Battle of San Juan Hill.

Each town with aspirations had its own "Opera House" or "Lyric Theatre." Most shows were vaudeville acts or low-budget traveling theatrical troupes that combined the occasional scene from Hamlet with jokes, songs, or magic tricks. Other acts featured performers in blackface.

A favorite of nearly all small towns was summer baseball. Towns put great stock in their ball teams and were not above hiring "ringers," or traveling professionals, to play key positions such as pitcher. Townships had their "farm teams," and each city fielded a team that played against rivals. Even largely immigrant communities developed teams. Children of immigrants often threw themselves into the game, which provided a bridge between the world of their parents and that of the native born. On the playing field, they would be judged by their skill, not their ethnicity, and they could play to boost the name of their community. Many tiny communities, without much economy, fielded legendary ball teams that consistently defeated rivals from larger, more successful towns.

Games were often raucous affairs, especially with no outfield fences and fiercely partisan local crowds whose relatives, spouses, and friends were on the field. Disputed calls at the plate might be settled with fists in the stands. A member of one team visiting a very small community recalled that when his home team opponents were introduced all nine had the same last name. But he knew they were in trouble when the umpire was introduced and he, too, had the same last name.

Summertime Chautauquas were a more refined form of entertainment that were especially popular in Protestant, Yankee-dominated small towns. They combined educational, political, and religious themes with art and culture in a way that was meant to be both entertaining and uplifting. Famous politicians, such as William Jennings Bryant, were often featured speakers. The program of events usually began with a children's hour in the morning, followed by a lecture that lasted until noon. After lunch there was a short musical interlude, followed by another lecture, dinner, a longer musical performance, and then another lecture. Lectures could be on virtually any topic, ranging from temperance to the state of the U.S. Merchant Marine to the customs of African pygmies or Greek islanders.

Perhaps the most enduring yearly activity has been "going to the lake" or "up to the cabin," or simply "up north." Time at the lake helped define what it meant to be a Minnesotan. Each summer, for a weekend, a week, a month, Minnesotans have gone to the state's bodies of water. What began in the 1920s as a fad among middle-class folk aping their wealthy neighbors gradually became an activity enjoyed by all. Their cabins could range from well-appointed summer homes to primitive shacks without running water or electricity. People went for many reasons: to get away from the city, to spend more time with family, to fish, or to commune with nature. In the days before easy transportation, such trips could mean being days from civilization. It was "roughing it" without the danger, a time when memories were made, of eating fish from the lake for dinner and berries with cream for dessert. In 1936, one young woman, Isabel Finnegan, wrote to a friend: "As I sit here and look out over the lake, I wonder if it will rain tonight. The sky is becoming a violently dark blue and the water looks soft as blue velvet."

Parts of outstate Minnesota developed a significant resort industry by the 1920s. As early as the 1890s, however, enterprising locals worked as guides, showing visitors the best places to hunt and fish. As urban expansion drew larger and larger crowds to urban amenities, the coming of the automobile allowed more people more access to scenic spots on Minnesota lakes beyond the Twin Cities. This helped increase contact between urban and rural Minnesota.

The small market towns of the rural Midwest were never the isolated backwaters portrayed by Sinclair Lewis and others. Virtually all were founded by the railroad and intimately connected to the outside world, to its markets and cultures. There has never been a time when such towns functioned as economically or culturally autonomous. Local stores always sold products made in distant factories, just as local stages and tents featured "Roman Hippodromes" and "Royal Japanese Equilibrists." The further the goods came and the more exotic they sounded, the better. Modernity was embraced and tradition downplayed. The fact that each market town developed its own distinctive attributes is largely thanks to the residents themselves, and to the diverse cultures and attitudes they brought with them or developed on their own.

Although there was no one "typical" small town, there were several varieties. River towns, which sprung up in the eastern part of the state along major, navigable rivers were older and better established. In the north, lumber camps functioned as temporary towns but often had little future. Towns built around mines or sawmills tended to be "company towns," often dominated by one or more large employers. Railroads established a variety of rural towns. Larger trade centers were either more centrally located (such as at the junction of two rail lines) or had other advantages (such as being the county seat). Their smaller neighbors were left with the table scraps.

From the beginning, many towns simply never matched the expectations and dreams of their promoters. Their town plans were drawn with dreams of lots for houses that were never built, businesses that never opened, schools that never had students, churches that never saw a congregation. Other towns reached their height of prosperity within a generation of settlement. Most towns were able to hold their own for a while, providing the surrounding area with a range of amenities: post office, bank, church, café, school, clothing store, furniture store. Sometimes, tiny hamlets without even a railroad, based around a church and containing perhaps just a saloon and a small store, were viable and lively places due to the social connections the church fostered, while towns that tried to "do it all" failed.

The successful towns were regional and local trade centers and of these there could only be a few. Due to location or some other advantage, these towns offered a wider range of stores and amenities and therefore attracted far more local farmers to sell their grain or to buy supplies and the latest new products. Towns that became regional trade centers gradually had a vampiric effect on the surrounding areas. Over the course of the twentieth century in rural Minnesota, the larger towns grew larger, the smaller places stagnated and then declined, and the countryside emptied.

The competition to be the lead city of a particular county or region was intense. This was especially the case when it came to public affairs. Many Minnesota counties saw bitter struggles over which town would be the county seat. Feeling that possession is nine-tenths of the law, one town even raided its rival during the night to seize the county records. In Lincoln County, Lake Benton and Ivanhoe's fight over the county seat went to the state supreme court in 1905, where it was decided in Ivanhoe's favor. In Lyon County, the rivalry between county seat Marshall and rival Tracy grew so fierce that proponents of

each town started spreading rumors that the other was infected with smallpox. In Tracy, several men boarded a Marshall-bound train and went through the passenger cars asking people where they were going. If some said Marshall, the men laughed and told them they would die because there was an epidemic raging there. Many passengers subsequently refused to get off at the Marshall stop and covered their mouths with cloths. When a county referendum over a new courthouse was decided in Marshall's favor, Marshallites met the train from Tracy with a brass band and jeering crowds. Such rivalries persisted for years, with each town's newspaper taking potshots at the neighbors. Sports became a primary way for smaller towns to get back at local rivals that were economically more successful.

Towns also competed in infrastructure building, with each one striving to be more modern and progressive. Whether it was schools, water, electricity, or telephones, each community strove to outdo its rivals. Small towns came to define themselves by infrastructure, and infrastructure in turn transformed life in town and country. Better roads meant easier travel to town, but they also made it easier for people to leave the countryside altogether. Electricity, too, was a major change. By the 1890s, most towns developed power plants, though few farms were wired. As one Minnesota newspaper editor noted in 1890, electric lights were so convenient that anyone "who tried them never [went] back to oil lamps." The editor continued:

> The oil used in the lamps is not all the expense of running them. Chimneys break, wicks and burners wear out, lamps break, grow old and get out of fashion, oil gets on the hired girl's hands and from there on your fried cakes and muffins, grease spots show up on your center table covers and sometimes on your carpets... occasionally the girl blows up your cook stove with a pint of it, and there is always lingering in your memory when away from home the tendency of the blamed old oil lamp to bust it [sic] chimney, blow up, and set the house on fire. You can't be a real right down simon-pure prize taking Christian and use oil lamps. That's why we quit. With electric lights half the annoyances of the home disappear. Your wife becomes an angel, the baby

never cries, shadows of all kinds are turned into beauties, and if you behave yourself in the daytime you are on the way to heaven.

Whether or not small-town Minnesotans made it to the Promised Land thanks to electricity is unknown, but increased electricity use sparked a boom of power-plant building in Minnesota. In the 1930s, the federal government would step in to help provide electricity to farms as well.

Each new infrastructure improvement was a new opportunity for local leaders to become boosters. What towns lacked in size and economic influence they tried to make up for in volume. By the 1920s and 1930s, however, some towns were pulling ahead of others economically. Although most had espoused the Progressive ethos of the times and the booster rhetoric that went with it, the world of rural Minnesota was not big enough for so many "new Chicagos."

Towns that had any state institution, be it a hospital, prison, or college, had an immediate advantage. Of equal importance was the ability to attract or develop processing plants. Nearly all small communities had their own co-operative creameries. Originally based on models developed in Denmark and introduced by Scandinavian immigrants, these creameries turned milk from local cows into butter, cream, or sometimes ice cream. Some cooperatives grew into farmer-owned corporations, such as Minnesota-based Land O'Lakes. In the long run, however, most of these small creameries did little to help small communities and nearby farmers survive hard times. A few towns developed larger processing plants. Hormel meats in Austin and turkey processor Jennie-O in Willmar were two typical examples. Louis Weiner, a Jewish immigrant peddler, opened Marshall Foods in the 1920s. All three of these companies helped their hometowns grow beyond the usual county seat town, insulating them to some degree against inevitable downturns in the farm economy.

HIGH-WATER MARK OF SMALL-TOWN MINNESOTA

Most of Minnesota's small communities reached their zenith in the 1920s, though most were able to maintain themselves more or less intact through the 1950s. Their leadership consisted largely of main street businessmen and professionals such as doctors, dentists, and lawyers. This group, however, could vary widely. Some small towns turned inward, becoming highly insular and even hostile to outsiders, which could include people from rival towns. Others remained fairly open and while newcomers were not always accepted socially, they were welcomed economically.

The main street store was a fixture of life in the state's small communities, but running them was never very easy. In spite of the image of stability projected by outside commentators, turnover rates for businesses in a small town were high. In many towns, as many as half of all businesses did not last five years. Those who stayed faced a constant balancing act. Keep too little inventory on hand and customers would go to competitors in bigger towns. Keep too much or too diverse inventory and it might not sell, leaving the merchant with big losses. The same was true with extending credit to customers. Extend too little and people would shop elsewhere. Too much and there was risk of bankruptcy if crops failed and farmers could not pay debts.

Merchants were a bridge, for better or worse, between the community and the larger world. They brought in goods from the outside and sold them to locals. At the same time, they tried to maintain their autonomy from the outside world and promote their own town and their own business.

In addition to businesses, voluntary groups and associations played an important leadership role in small communities. In particular, women's clubs were a crucial element of small-town life. Though often satirized as intellectually vapid tea drinkers, the members of women's clubs were more likely to be quite sophisticated and were often the best educated people around. One women's club, the Current News Club of Marshall, left detailed records of their discussion topics, which included current research in the social sciences, British and German literature, the works of Ralph Waldo Emerson, and the history of Latin America. These clubs also played a crucial role as local reformers, spurring changes in public health and education, and, of course, the right of women to vote. The fact that nearly every small town had a library and at least one park was usually due to women's clubs.

Famous Minnesotans: Judy Garland

Born June 10, 1922 as Frances Ethel Gumm, Grand Rapids, Minn. Died June 22, 1969, Los Angeles.

One of the most recognized American actresses of the mid twentieth century, Judy Garland was born in northern Minnesota as Frances Ethel Gumm, but her family moved to Los Angeles when she was quite young. With her sisters, Garland was part of the Gumm Sisters' singing act. The sisters first appeared in a Hollywood film in 1929 when Garland was seven. The act later changed its name to the Garland Sisters and Frances Gumm became Judy Garland. After appearing in a number of films with her sisters, Garland received her own contract with MGM studios in 1935. She was chosen for the lead role of Dorothy in *The Wizard of Oz* in 1939 due to her looks, acting, and singing ability. Garland starred in some 40 films, including *Meet Me in St. Louis*, *Judgement at Nuremburg*, and *A Star is Born*, and received a special Academy Award in 1939. Garland's personal life was rather less successful, with a series of five marriages beginning at the age of 19. She had two daughters, Liza Minnelli, by husband/director Vincente Minnelli, and Lorna Luft, by producer/husband Sid Luft. After her last major film in 1963, she embarked on a short career on television. The 1960s were not kind to Garland, professionally or personally, and she died in 1969 at the age of 47.

The seeds of decline in rural Minnesota were planted from the start. Even in the age of horse and wagon, there were too many towns, spaced too closely together, competing for the business of the same farmers, who themselves were not too economically successful. In the 1930s, the problems became too big to ignore. As the nation's economy went into freefall following the Wall Street crash, farmers suffered more than most. The worst hit were those who had taken out loans during the relatively good years of the 1920s. As small-town banks and stores faced a run on deposits, many tried to call in loans and credit extended to farmers. When farmers could not pay, the threat of foreclosure became a reality. As families started to lose their farms to foreclosure, a wave of farm protest engulfed large parts of Minnesota.

The Farmer's Holiday movement was the most effective and most radical farm protest in American history and it had particular strength in western Minnesota. Holiday members staged penny auctions. Members would show up en masse at a farm foreclosure auction and bid one penny for anything offered for sale. Those who tried to bid anything more were beaten up or intimidated into silence. Another tactic for stopping foreclosures was to grab the local sheriff or judge and hold them prisoner. Holiday activist John Bosch recalled that "This particular day in Montevideo they were foreclosing in federal court. A U.S. marshal was there and I bet I had about 10,000 farmers there." Bosch tried to convince authorities to call off the sale. The marshal answered:

> "Well," he said, "it doesn't make any difference how much I agree with you, I must proceed with the sale."… Well, out in the hall where you couldn't identify somebody, somebody would holler "Let the son of a bitch out here and we'll cut a hole in the ice and push him down twice and pull him up once." Somebody else would say "Let's tie him with one hind leg behind the car and haul him back to St. Paul," and this type of thing and he [the marshal] was white as a sheet.

In 1933, with the election of Franklin D. Roosevelt as president and the passage of anti-foreclosure measures in some states, the Holiday movement tried to up the ante by means of a farm strike. Farmers were supposed to withhold their products from the processing plants until they got better prices. But the response from farmers was lukewarm. In the fall of 1933, the Holiday tried to shut down processing plants throughout western and southwestern Minnesota, leading to some of the most dramatic confrontations. In Montevideo, farmers occupied a local creamery, making it their headquarters. To the south, in Marshall, the Swift and Co. packing plant refused to shut down, and on November 10, 1933, some 1,100 farmers arrived to do just that. When the local sheriff tried to turn fire hoses on the crowd, a riot ensued. The farmers disarmed the sheriff and his deputies, chopped

Must-See Sites: Science Museum of Minnesota, St. Paul

Science Museum of Minnesota is a fun way to learn about science and the natural world, with exhibits for both adults and children. The museum's collections include archeology and ethnology; mammalogy, entomology, and ornithology; vertebrate and invertebrate paleontology; and river and stream ecology and watershed biology. Its 1.75 million artifacts and specimens are worldwide in scope and range in size from microscopic spores to dinosaurs and whales. The museum's Omnitheatre has a changing array of shows that allow visitors to feel right in the middle of a pod of whales, to explore the Antarctic, or see life inside a space station.

Contact: (651) 221-9444; Web: www.sci.mus.mn.us

Location: The Science Museum of Minnesota on the bluffs of the Mississippi River at 120 W. Kellogg Blvd, St. Paul.

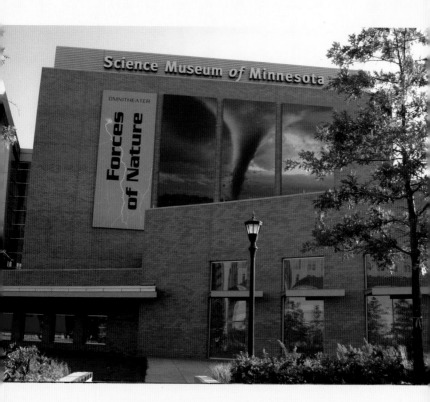

Entrance to the Science Museum of Minnesota

apart the fire hoses, and proceeded to smash the police cars with rocks. Only intervention by a local state senator prevented serious violence. The city's plants shut down, but the victory for the Farmer's Holiday was short lived. Slightly better economic conditions and the radicalism of the movement caused its appeal to fade quickly. Never again would farmers have such strength.

Despite the periodic farm protests, the 1930s saw the rise of the small processing towns. People moved from farms and very small towns to larger towns and cities. Regional trade centers gained population. In a kind of economic vampirism, larger communities sucked population and wealth from the nearby areas, but they in turn lost to even bigger cities. Lead cities also had the clout and the political savvy to seek and win increased government spending for projects large and small. The Works Progress Administration (WPA) and the Civilian Conservation Corps (CCC), part of Roosevelt's New Deal, helped to transform outstate Minnesota both through its building projects—roads, bridges, post offices, airports, and parks—and by increasing the mobility of rural residents, offering them wage jobs in new locations.

Infrastructure, too, had a transforming impact. Better roads allowed farmers to get their crops to market faster, but also allowed farm families more ready access to the cities. One of the most important but overlooked New Deal programs was the Rural Electrification Administration (REA). By providing inexpensive electricity to Minnesota farms, REA not only transformed the technology of agriculture by allowing more and greater mechanization, but also changed how rural people saw themselves and their world. Many still remember the day they got electricity and how the darkness of the night changed as each farm in succession lit its outdoor lights for the first time. In less than ten years nearly all farms in the state had access to electricity.

In addition to improving roads and the advent of rural electricity, the radio created a third transformation. Radio linked rural and small-town Minnesota into the developing mass culture of America. It began to break down the cultural autonomy of rural communities as it increased awareness of the larger world. Prior to radio, few rural Minnesotans listened to country/bluegrass music, which was a largely southern musical tradition. Through radio, however, such music was marketed to rural people as "rural music." Radio and phonographs, however, also provided a new venue for more familiar "ethnic" music, such as the polka, which also took on new importance. The value of tradition suddenly seemed less important. Things deemed "modern" had a luster that tradition could not match. How rural people entertained themselves and how they related to the larger world was also transformed by small-town movie theaters. New ideas of style, of physical attractiveness, or of what it meant to be an American, were transmitted from the big cities into the most remote corners of rural Minnesota with a speed and an impact that had been unimaginable a generation before.

The economic boom of the late 1940s and 1950s helped outstate Minnesota just as it helped everyone, but the effects were not always even. Processing towns and the Iron Range fared well, but smaller towns stagnated and declined. Renewed efforts to build an effective political movement of farmers failed. The high-water mark of rural Minnesota had come and gone. For those who had served in the U.S. armed forces during World War II and had seen the bright lights of a larger world that included London, Rome, or Paris, it was often hard to return home. One woman remember how her brother came back from the service and would pace the kitchen floor of their farm house as if the place he had grown up in had suddenly become too small. He soon moved to the big city and left the farming life behind forever. There were many who would do the same.

Must-See Sites: Ironworld Discovery Center, Chisholm

Commemorating the history and cultures of Minnesota's Iron Range, Ironworld Discovery Center allows visitors to discover Old World customs and traditions through living history interpreters, still and interactive exhibits, and colorful displays. Visitors can also sample delicious dishes from around the world, trace their roots, enjoy different cultural events and entertainment, ride a genuine trolley along the edge of Glen Mine, and visit Pellet Pete's miniature golf course. The Iron Range Research Center is open year round for genealogists and historians.

Contact: (218) 254-7959 or (800) 372-6437; Web: www.ironworld.com
Location: Hwy 169 West, Chisholm.

9

New Places, New Faces

In the decades following World War II, Minnesota, like the rest of the nation, enjoyed an unprecedented economic boom. The state's residents could with justice claim to have the good life. Minnesota's economy, while still heavily dependent on agriculture, relied less and less on farmers. The state's processing industry shielded it from problems on the farm. Farming was also balanced with manufacturing and mining, though unlike many midwestern states, Minnesota was never so dependent on manufacturing that it was affected by the "rust belt" syndrome of the 1970s and 1980s. A well-educated workforce proved highly adaptable, innovative, and entrepreneurial, while amenities such as parks, lakes, resorts, and wilderness drew tourists in search of relaxation and migrants looking for greener pastures. A progressive liberalism promised social peace and an improved quality of life. Everyone could be a winner.

Minnesota Liberalism

Throughout the 1950s, 1960s, and 1970s, the state was dominated by giants of the Democratic party such as Hubert Humphrey and later Walter Mondale, both prominent in national politics. The state DFL took the governor's seat in 1952 behind C. Elmer Anderson, who passed the torch to Orville Freeman. When Freeman became secretary of agriculture under President Kennedy, Karl Rolvaag became the next DFLer to win the governor's seat. After Rolvaag came Wendall Anderson, who was famous for appearing on the cover of *Time* holding a just-caught fish with the headline "The Good Life in Minnesota." Thus, for more than two decades, the state was largely run by a group of leaders with a common vision of the "good life" that included a mix of rural self-reliance and a healthy role for government in planning a safe, clean, well-run state.

In the 1950s and 1960s, urban areas boomed while small towns prospered. Even in the smaller communities, the postwar baby boom hid the reality of emigration, at least for a time. The core urban areas expanded as new suburbs incorporated and began to develop as communities in their own right. The wartime boom on the Iron Range, which saw massive extractions of iron ore, continued after the fighting in Europe and the Pacific subsided. Taconite (a low-grade ore) increasingly became a substitute for the depleted higher-grade ores. The new taconite-processing industry resulted in the building of entirely new company towns, such as Silver Bay on the shores of Lake Superior.

Throughout the postwar decades, Minnesota's population grew steadily, from just under 3 million in 1950 to just over 4 million in 1980. Migration into the state by people in search of jobs and opportunity kept pace almost exactly with migration out of the state, and births outnumbered deaths. In this way the population remained relatively stable and was able to grow slowly. Those immigrating came most frequently from neighboring states, while those leaving the state often moved to one of the coasts, especially to the west coast and the south. The number of new immigrants was not great, although Minnesota was home to some postwar refugees from Europe, including Jewish and Polish Holocaust survivors and those fleeing communist persecution in eastern Europe. The African American population also grew due to migration from the south and from places such as Chicago and Kansas City.

Although many Minnesotans continued to speak languages other than English at home or in their religious communities, the use of English increased. Young people who had served in the armed forces or who had worked in wartime industries had formative experiences outside of their home communities where English was the norm. When other languages were spoken, they were most often interspersed with English. It was not uncommon for those who grew up in such a bilingual atmosphere to start a sentence in one language and finish in another. The postwar boom, however, meant that the children and grandchildren of immigrants could move into the middle class, and the price for all too many was the submerging of their diverse cultural backgrounds.

Must-See Sites: Zippel Bay State Park, Williams

The park is located on the shores of Lake of the Woods, one of the world's largest lakes. Because of its size, the lake freezes much later than most lakes and remains ice-covered much later in the spring. In the spring hear the ice as it is stressed by wind and compression. During the winter, visitors will be treated to a view of the intricate ice forms on rocks and shore. The mood of the lake is always changing, from three-foot-high crashing waves, approaching storms and lightning flashes, to an eerie stillness with faint sounds from a thousand raucous gulls, out of sight in the lake's interior. The 3,000-acre park offers a swimming beach on the big lake with white sand beaches, a marina in Zippel Bay, and a stone jetty providing access to Lake of the Woods and safe passage off the lake. Watch for sandhill cranes and piping plovers. The park offers drive-in campsites and a group camp.

Contact: (218) 783-6252;Web: www.dnr.state.mn.us/state_parks/ or www.stayatmnparks.com

Location: From the west end of Baudette, take Highway 172, 10 miles north to County Road 8. Go west on 8 to the park entrance.

At the same time, overt prejudice against many groups declined. In Minneapolis, long a bastion of exclusion against Jews and Catholics, old barriers began to fall in the 1950s, especially under the leadership of Mayor Hubert H. Humphrey. African Americans continued to suffer discrimination in terms of housing and jobs. Restrictive housing covenants and informal prejudice against Jews and other groups as well continued even into the 1960s. Nevertheless, such discrimination was increasingly less and less tolerated by most Minnesotans.

If ethnicity became less emphasized in some areas, it became more so in others. Servicemen returning from Europe had acquired new tastes and better communication, and transportation began to change what appeared everyday on Minnesota's dinner tables. There had been a time before large-scale immigration from southern Europe that the tomato had been considered an exotic, foreign food. Now it became a staple of table and garden. Along with it came spaghetti and pizza. An Italian American from Duluth named Jeno Paulucci turned ethnic food into a major business, with brands like Chung King, Jeno's Pizza Rolls, and Totino's pizza. As his autobiography noted, "Only in America would it be possible for a man with a name like Jeno Francisco Paulucci, son of poor Italian immigrants, to get rich selling Chinese food in a Scandinavian region."

But it was not only Italian Americans who got in on the craze for new food for a new era. Marvin Schwan, the son of a German immigrant, began marketing ice cream to farm families who had acquired the essential modern luxury of an ice box. His company, Marshall-based Schwan's Sales Enterprises, later branched out into frozen pizza, creating national brands like Red Baron and Tony's. Thus did a state with a relatively small Italian population become a major interpreter of Italian cuisine—of sorts—for average Americans.

The era of ethnic enclaves had bred specific local cuisines with their own aromas and flavors. The postwar era saw an erosion of those differences. The University of Minnesota extension service through its local field agents not only promoted modern production agriculture, but also new foods that would provide simple, filling meals that would not tie farm women to the kitchen and garden all day. Although "tater-tot hotdish" and the various creative uses of JELL-O of the stereotypical Lutheran church supper may be considered "traditional" Minnesota fare by some wags, they are dishes that rely heavily on processed or canned ingredients and became popular only after the war.

Minnesota's changes in eating habits reflected broader changes in the state as a whole. Contrary to popular belief, women's participation in the workforce grew in the 1950s and women adopted new social roles as well. Although the women's study clubs of the early twentieth century declined in vigor, new organizations, including block clubs, veteran's auxiliary groups, and parent-teacher associations provided important venues for women to work for the good of their communities and families, and provided an introduction to grassroots politics and decisionmaking.

The state's population, while never static, had new opportunities for travel and mobility thanks to growing prosperity and better transportation. New and better roads, especially interstate highways, made urban centers and larger towns more accessible to rural people, while lakeside cabins were within ever easier reach of urbanites. Vacations to other parts of the country became more common. If roads took people to new destinations, they also brought the world to one's doorstep. Thanks to inexpensive fuel and good roads, overnight trucking became increasingly economical, allowing even the most perishable food products to be shipped to stores in small communities. Several Minnesota entrepreneurs led the way. While German-American Marvin Schwan brought frozen treats to farm families, Polish immigrant Stan Wasie pioneered overnight shipping with his Minneapolis-based Merchants Trucking Company.

Perhaps the most crucial element in the state's postwar growth was the expansion of college and university enrollment. The G. I. Bill, along with greater prosperity in general, allowed more and more students, both men and women, to get higher education. The University of Minnesota was a major beneficiary of these changes. Its enrollment increased steadily in the 1950s and 1960s. It added new programs and gained a national reputation for research.

Minnesota's insatiable demand for higher education can best be seen in the development of the state college system. Five of the seven schools now in existence (Bemidji, Mankato, Moorhead, St. Cloud, and Winona) began as teacher's colleges designed to educate teachers for the state's many urban and rural districts. In the postwar era, they became full-fledged four-year colleges, and between 1940 and 1970 their combined enrollments grew more than six fold. In the 1960s, Marshall gained the state's sixth college (Southwest State) and in 1972 an urban school, Metro State, opened with facilities in Minneapolis and St. Paul. In the late 1970s, all these colleges were renamed universities. The two largest, St. Cloud State University and Mankato State University, had achieved enrollments of over 10,000 each by the early 1970s.

The numerous, small private religious colleges in the state also grew in size, though more slowly. These institutions

Famous Minnesotans:
Hubert H. Humphrey

Born May 27, 1911, Wallace, S.D.
Died Jan. 13, 1978, Waverly, Minn.

Hubert Horatio Humphrey was the most important politician to emerge from Minnesota's liberal tradition. The son of a South Dakota storekeeper, Humphrey attended the University of Minnesota and by the 1940s was recognized as a rising star of Minnesota politics. In 1945 he became the youngest mayor of Minneapolis. In this role he was instrumental in making the city a leader in fair employment practices and in ending informal discrimination against Jews and Catholics. He also played a key role in the merger of the Democratic and Farmer–Labor parties. In 1948 Humphrey was elected to the U.S. Senate and soon became well-known for his brilliant speaking ability and his commitment to civil rights, for which his exuberance and willingness to take a stand earned him the nickname "the Happy Warrior." His first major legislative proposal was later enacted in 1965 as the Medicare bill for medical assistance for the elderly. Reelected to the Senate in 1954 and 1960, Humphrey became a leader of the Democratic party, during which time he was elected assistant majority leader. In 1964 he was elected vice-president of the United States on the ticket with Lyndon B. Johnson. During the divisive 1968 presidential campaign, Humphrey was able to retain the loyalty of most delegates to the controversial Chicago Democratic convention and was nominated for the presidency. Nevertheless, he lost to Richard Nixon by a narrow margin. He was reelected to the Senate in 1970 and 1976. In 1976 he was stricken with cancer and died in 1978.

specialized in creating more prestigious degrees and, as they sought to attract the best students and move public money, they gradually secularized. This trend was most pronounced in colleges associated with the mainline Protestant denominations, but all experienced secularization to one degree or another. Colleges such as Macalester, Hamline, St. Olaf, Carleton, and St. Thomas developed national reputations as undergraduate liberal arts institutions.

SUBURBANIZATION

The most visible sign of the state's expanding and upwardly mobile population was the growth of suburbs around the Twin Cities following World War II. Farming villages and lakeside resort communities quickly urbanized and some were soon counted among the state's largest communities. In 1940 Edina had less than 6,000 residents, but it became the "golden west" as Minneapolis's well-to-do moved out of the city, and by 1970 its population had increased seven fold. Nearby St. Louis Park, a favored destination of many of Minneapolis's upwardly mobile Jews, grew by almost the same proportion, reaching nearly 50,000 by 1970. By the same token, large unincorporated areas developed as new cities. Incorporation dates tell the story of this expansion. Roseville, now an inner-ring suburb, incorporated in 1948 with 4,589 residents. By 1970, within one generation, its population stood at nearly 35,000, a six-fold increase. To the south of Minneapolis, Bloomington incorporated in 1953 and by 1960 had over 50,000 residents, placing it in the top five Minnesota cities. By 1990, its population topped 86,000, surpassing Duluth to become the state's third largest city. Other new suburban cities followed with equally astounding growth, including Brooklyn Park (1954), Mendota Heights (1956), Eden Prairie (1962), Burnsville (1964), Cottage Grove (1965), Woodbury (1967), Apple Valley (1968), and Eagan (1972).

As upwardly mobile Minnesotans sought ever-greener pastures to build the home of their dreams on a large lot, the suburbs came to include such old historic towns as Hastings and Stillwater, which simultaneously struggled to reap the economic advantages of growth while attempting to maintain their distinctive character. With good roads and fair weather, St. Cloud was an hour away on I-94, a reasonable

drive for some. By 1990 a corridor of growth along the interstate linked St. Cloud to the larger metro area. Even cities like Mankato were not out of driving distance for some commuters. Commuting times rose year by year.

As the suburbs expanded, the core urban areas stagnated. Minneapolis's population peaked in 1950 at 521,718, while St. Paul hit its height a decade later with 313,411. Thereafter, both cities experienced a slow, steady loss of population. This occurred despite—or even because of—modest efforts at "urban renewal" that may have removed some eyesores but took the community along with them. The arrival of the interstate highway system in

Macalaster College campus, St. Paul

the Twin Cities hastened the exodus. The new freeways provided easy commutes from the suburbs. The interstates also broke up long-standing neighborhoods. In St. Paul, the historic African American neighborhood of Rondo largely disappeared beneath I-94 and in North Minneapolis it went through the middle of an old Jewish and Polish district. Old residents died or moved out and their children went to the suburbs. Those who took their place did not always share the same sense of place or community.

The most visible symbol of this new way of urban living was the shopping mall. Perfectly suited to the suburbs and to keeping shoppers out of inclement Minnesota weather, malls flourished in the Twin Cities as perhaps nowhere else. Even smaller cities developed their own malls by the 1980s. Yet the biggest of them all did not arrive until the early 1990s. Opened in 1992 on the site of the old Met Stadium, Bloomington's Mall of America is the largest entertainment and retail complex in the U.S. Welcoming over 42 million guests each year, the Mall of America is the nation's most visited attraction.

Declining population in the core cities notwithstanding, the Twin Cities took on hallmarks of a major urban center. For many, this was symbolized by the arrival of new professional sports teams. By the 1950s, professional sports were seen as a major source of civic pride and one of those amenities that made an urban center something more than a flyover zone. In 1955 local civic leaders tried to anticipate winning sports franchises by building Metropolitan Stadium in Bloomington. In this they were hoping to reap rewards similar to those in Milwaukee

Must-See Sites: Mall of America, Bloomington

Opened in 1992 on the site of the old Met Stadium, Bloomington's Mall of America is the largest entertainment and retail complex in the U.S. Total traffic is between 35 to 42 million visits yearly. It employs more than 12,000 people. Seven Yankee Stadiums would fit inside the mall. Mall of America's 13,300 short tons of steel is nearly twice the amount in the Eiffel Tower. Walking distance around one level of Mall of America is .57 of a mile. Spending 10 minutes in every store would take a shopper more than 86 hours. The mall has over 525 specialty stores, 4 national department stores, over 50 restaurants, 7 nightclubs, 14 movie theaters, and more.

Contact: (952) 883-8800; www.mallofamerica.com
Location: South of 494 on Cedar Avenue, Bloomington.

where downtown business jumped dramatically with the arrival of the Braves in 1953. By 1959 local businessmen were working hard to create a professional football team. The following year, Minnesota got its football team, which it named the Vikings in a bow to local Scandinavian pride. They avoid rivalry between the two "twin" cities by naming the team after the state.

As Viking football was set to get underway in 1961, the state got a surprise gift. The poorly performing Washington Senators, a franchise founded in 1900, announced they were moving to Minnesota at the end of the 1960 season. The team was renamed the Twins and both teams now filled the bill at Met Stadium, which for Minnesotans of a certain age was the scene of their first live pro sports experience. Professional sports drew together Minnesotans from all parts of the state. They also drew fans from other states, particularly western Wisconsin, northern Iowa, and the eastern Dakotas.

Both new sports teams faced the problems of expansion teams. The Twins reached the World Series in 1965, but lost to the Dodgers. They fielded respectable teams into the 1970s behind stars like Harmon Killebrew, Bob Allison, and Tony Oliva. It was not until the late 1980s and a change of ownership that the Twins became a serious contender. In 1988, fielding stars like Kirby Puckett and Kent Hrbek, Minnesota won its first major league sports championship when the Twins beat the St. Louis Cardinals in the World Series. In 1991 they repeated the performance in a close seven-game series with the favored Atlanta Braves. The Vikings had their chances at glory as well. In 1969 the team reached Super Bowl IV but was beaten by Kansas City. In the 1970s, Coach Bud Grant built a powerful team that dominated the Central Division of the NFC. With "the Purple People Eater" Defense and with an offense lead by quarterback Fran Tarkenton, the Vikes were especially formidable at home during the winter where the stoic Grant shut off sideline heaters, leaving Sun Belt teams to freeze. In 1973 the Vikings played in Super Bowl VIII, but were trounced by Miami. The next year, the team reached Super Bowl IX, but lost to Pittsburgh. In 1976 the Vikings became the first team in NFL history to lose four Super Bowls, this time Super Bowl XI, when they lost to Oakland.

Minnesota's changing face affected different groups in different ways. Descendants of the state's original inhabitants are a particularly poignant study in contrasts. Following World War II, many Native Americans began to migrate to the Twin Cities and Duluth in search of jobs that simply did not exist on the reservations. By the 1980s, Minneapolis had one of the larger urban concentrations of Native Americans in the United States. The city became a center of the American Indian Movement (AIM) and developed a variety of other institutions as well, including a newspaper, *The Circle* (established in 1980), and schools such as Heart of the Earth Survival School and Little Red Schoolhouse. On the reservations, however, life remained difficult, despite some efforts at economic development. Unemployment rates were far in excess of the state average and income levels and living standards were below it. Chemical dependency remained a major problem.

Yet significant changes were in the offing for the state's Native Americans. A new generation of activists had begun pushing for a change in attitudes in the 1970s, but it was two developments of the mid to late 1980s that would have the biggest impact. The most significant was the development of Native American casino gambling. The state's first Native American casino opened in 1987, at the Lower Sioux Community near Morton. For a few short years, Jackpot Junction was the largest casino between Atlantic City and Las Vegas, and tour groups from as far away as Chicago arrived for gambling. Other tribes in Minnesota and the Midwest followed suit.

As new money flowed into Native American communities, new opportunities and new problems arose. Management of casino profits varied widely. Some communities invested in infrastructure, community centers, education, and jobs. The Mille Lacs Band of Ojibwe opened their own museum to portray their history and culture in their own terms for the first time. Other bands merely split the proceeds among all members. In some cases, people who not long before had lived without running water were collecting monthly checks of $2,000. Conflicts arose over who was a band member and thus entitled to the profits.

With money came greater power and greater confidence. Native American casinos were suddenly able to

Ethnic and Racial Groups in Minnesota by Size, 2000[*]

German   1,806,650
Norwegian   850,742
Irish   552,172
Swedish   486,507
English/British   321,738
French/French Canadian   262,203
Polish   240,405
African American/Black   171,731
Italian   111,270
Czech/Czechoslovakian   101,702
Dutch   99,944
Finnish   99,388
Mexican   95,613
Danish   88,924
Hmong & Laotian   64,577
Scottish   62,152
American Indian/Native American   54,967
"Scandinavian"   52,085
Scots-Irish   46,370
Russian   35,513
Swiss   23,140
Welsh   21,677
Vietnamese   18,824
Austrian   17,483
Asian Indian   16,887
Chinese   16,060
Belgian   15,627
Ukrainian   14,356
Arab   13,923
Korean   12,584
Hungarian/Magyar   12,279
Somali   11,164
Greek   10,619
Slovene   10,420

*Includes groups with 10,000 or more
reported members only.

hire lobbyists and gain access to the corridors of power that had for so long been closed to native peoples. Local legislators, conscious of the economic development potential of casinos, started to pay attention to what Native American leaders had to say. As this transformation began to take effect, Native American activists began to re-examine old treaties from the nineteenth century, uncovering clauses that had never been honored by state and federal governments. Ojibwe bands in Minnesota and Wisconsin brought successful lawsuits to regain hunting and fishing rights promised under these treaties but long ignored in practice. This led to conflicts with local outdoors groups and resort owners who feared a loss of business and a loss of fish and wildlife populations. Although this conflict was far more intense in Wisconsin, in Minnesota fears of the destruction of wildlife populations proved premature.

NEWCOMERS

New groups also made their presence felt in the state. After national immigration laws were changed in 1965, new immigrants began to make their way to Minnesota. At first these numbers were small. War and communist takeovers in Indochina, however, would change this. Following the fall of Saigon in 1975, many Minnesota communities hosted refugees from Vietnam. Social service agencies that resettled these refugees dispersed them widely, placing small groups in towns and cities throughout the state. The Vietnamese presence in many towns was short-lived, as they migrated to join relatives elsewhere and reunite their scattered families. Yet a more permanent Vietnamese community developed in the Twin Cities, which also included some ethnic Chinese from southeast Asia. With a significant proportion of educated people, these new arrivals proved highly entrepreneurial and many soon opened their own businesses.

Following the Vietnamese were Hmong immigrants. Originally from the hills and mountains of Laos, the Hmong had fought courageously for the anti-communist cause in southeast Asia and were notable for saving the lives of many downed U.S. pilots. For this they suffered severe persecution, causing large numbers to flee their homeland. Many came to live in the United States and quite a few arrived in

Famous Minnesotans: Walter F. Mondale

Born Jan. 5, 1928, Ceylon, Minn.

The son of a Methodist minister and a lawyer by training, Walter F. Mondale became active in Democratic politics in Minnesota during his college days at the University of Minnesota. Mondale worked on Hubert H. Humphrey's campaign for mayor of Minneapolis and in 1960 managed the reelection campaign of Gov. Orville Freeman, who appointed Mondale the state's attorney general. He was reelected to the position in 1960 and 1962. In 1964 he was chosen to fill the remainder of Humphrey's senate seat when the latter became vice president. Mondale was reelected to the Senate in 1966 and 1972. Like his mentor Humphrey, Mondale was a staunch supporter of Great-Society liberalism, continuing a Minnesota tradition. In 1976 he was chosen as the Democratic vice-presidential candidate behind Jimmy Carter and elected vice president that year. He became one of Carter's most trusted advisors. Following Ronald's Reagan's election in 1980, Mondale returned to politics as the Democratic nominee for president in 1984, choosing Geraldine Ferraro as his running mate, the first woman nominated for such a high office. Nevertheless, Mondale proved unable to defeat the popular Reagan and lost in a landslide. During the Clinton administration, Mondale was named U.S. ambassador to Japan. Following a term as ambassador, Mondale retired from active politics, except for a brief and unsuccessful bid for U.S. Senator when he stood in place of the late Paul Wellstone in 2003.

Minnesota. The initial group of arrivals in the 1980s was bolstered by a second group of Hmong, many of whom migrated from California in the 1990s. St. Paul became a particularly favored location for these newcomers.

The Hmong had greater difficulty adjusting to life in a new land than had the Vietnamese. The written form of the Hmong language had only existed since 1958 and many of the older immigrants were functionally illiterate and more than a few were permanently disabled due to the war. While some Hmong opened their own businesses, adults usually took low or medium-skill wage jobs. Although the community put a strong emphasis on education, the urban street culture seduced its share of Hmong youth who, like other immigrant youth before them, felt both alienated and attracted by mainstream culture, but also loyal to the

Northern skyline of downtown Minneapolis

culture of their elders. Nevertheless, community groups and outside agencies made a major effort to adapt Hmong traditions to the new reality, beginning the process of successfully creating a hybrid Hmong-American culture.

Opportunities in higher education and in Minnesota's growing technology-based industries brought many immigrants from India and the Middle East as well. Many arrived as college students, often taking degrees in technical fields. Quite a few stayed in the state, finding jobs and opportunities unavailable elsewhere. With little fanfare, Minnesota's population of Asian Indians grew to nearly 17,000 in 2000, exceeding that of Chinese Americans, whose history in the state stretched back much further. Groups from the Middle East were more diverse. The older Lebanese community continued as the largest, but in the 1980s and 1990s great numbers of Egyptians and Iranians, as well as smaller groups of Turks and Afghans, found a home in the North Star State. In general, these groups were characterized by high levels of education and dominated by professionals and small businesspeople.

Civil war and famine in east Africa brought a different wave of refugees and immigrants to Minnesota in the 1980s and 1990s. People from Ethiopia were the first to arrive, with Oromo constituting the largest group, though there were also Eritreans and others. The first Oromo community group, the Oromo Support Committee, was active by 1985. These groups were relatively small compared to the much larger wave of Somalis that arrived in the 1990s. Somalis were the first Muslim ethnic group that was large enough and traditional enough to be visible to the majority of Minnesotans. The largest settlement of Somalis occurred in Minneapolis, but they also found homes in St. Paul, Rochester, Worthington, and Marshall.

The largest of the new immigrant groups was not really new. Mexican immigrants had come to Minnesota as early as the 1910s and the first permanent community in West St. Paul came into being in the 1920s. Yet the late 1980s and 1990s brought a new wave of Mexicans and Mexican Americans to the state. Following trails well worn by previous generations of migrant laborers, who had been coming each year to work in the sugar beet fields of northern and central Minnesota, a new generation of Mexicans began to find better-paying work in small-town meat processing plants. From there, these immigrants moved into other job categories in both rural and urban Minnesota.

The new immigrants, both legal and illegal, came from diverse parts of Mexico and even included indigenous people from states like Chiapas. However, many of the new arrivals were actually Americans, coming from towns on the Texas side of the U.S.–Mexican border. Being within a few days' drive of their original homes set these immigrants apart from the Hmong and Somali immigrants who arrived at the same time. Many of the Mexican and Mexican-American newcomers saw their sojourn in Minnesota as a temporary one. Their goal was to earn money to support a family back home. A family member with a low-wage job in rural Minnesota could help a family work its way out of poverty. Like many European immigrants of an earlier time, some Mexican immigrants doubtless arrived with the intention of going back, but soon put down roots in Minnesota and decided to stay.

From a cultural standpoint, immigration and ethnicity expressed themselves in new ways. Websites and local-access TV programs took their place besides cultural journals, newspapers, newsletters, and book publishing as ways to preserve and sustain cultures in diaspora. Alongside its mainstream cultural achievements, Minnesota was home to national publications devoted to literature produced by Arab Americans, Korean Americans, and Hmong Americans, to name a few. International film festivals and a seemingly endless parade of new restaurants appealed to residents old and new. Older, more established ethnic communities joined in a rapidly burgeoning interest in genealogy that led to the creation of active ethnic genealogical groups.

The new immigrants of the 1980s and 1990s were attracted to Minnesota primarily by the jobs created by the state's growing economy. In the late 1990s, employment plummeted and many employers had difficulty filling low-skill positions. This was particularly the case in many small-town processing plants.

The Loss of the Small Towns

The arrival of new immigrants in the state's smaller towns threw the demographic changes occurring in these communities into dramatic relief. In the 1970s, the price of farmland skyrocketed and farmers were encouraged to expand their operations. "Get big or get out," was the mantra of the day. High land prices gave farmers equity to borrow money and banks were more than willing to lend. Better production and more land under cultivation meant bigger crops, which meant lower prices for what farmers

Must-See Sites:
Children's Museum, St. Paul

Fun meets learning at the Minnesota Children's Museum. Children ages 6 months through 10 years and adult guests can explore six galleries packed with extraordinary hands-on adventures and interactive displays. Kids can take the stage in a music studio, burrow through a giant anthill, get nose-to-beak with a turtle, or operate a big crane. Two changing galleries host new and traveling exhibits throughout the year.

Contact: (651) 225-6000 or (651) 225-6001; Web: www.mcm.org

Location: At the corner of Seventh and Wabasha Streets, downtown St. Paul.

produced. As prices fell, land values also dropped dramatically, leaving many family farmers heavily in debt, and sparking the farm crisis of the early 1980s. Although some farms were foreclosed on, the more common fate of the family was of an older generation of farmers whose children abandoned the farm by going to college and joining the white-collar workforce rather than struggling against such long odds. Farms grew still larger and the number of farmers fewer.

Fewer farmers meant fewer customers for the small-town businesses, and competition for retail trade sharpened. Regional trade centers—mostly towns over 7,500 people—were able to hold their own or grow slightly. In many cases, however, the growth of towns was vampiric: They merely drew population from an emptying countryside and dying country hamlets. The countless smaller towns lost their fight for survival. Businesses failed and schools consolidated. Most of these towns ceased to be fully functioning communities. Their aging populations suffered natural decline (a condition where deaths outnumber births) as well as emigration. A few activists staged noisy demonstrations, and policy makers and grant makers drew up perfect paper plans to save the family farm or save Main Street, but for most places the handwriting was already on the wall.

Regional trade centers were themselves perched close to the margin between survival and decline. To create new jobs was the goal of every community economic development plan of the 1980s. Tax breaks and other incentives lured many meat-processing companies to establish plants in smaller communities as the industry decentralized. Yet these new plants did not produce the kinds of jobs local leaders had envisioned. Their schools were producing graduates with ambitions to go to college and become doctors, lawyers, or business people. The number of people willing to take jobs paying from $5 to $7.50 per hour was small. As a result, companies recruited heavily to bring Mexican and Mexican Americans, as well as some Somali and Hmong immigrants, to work in these plants.

Local residents often greeted the arrival of so many newcomers in so short a time with dismay. The small towns had seen nothing like it since the influx of immigrants a century before. The immigrants were highly mobile, and meatpacking plants sometimes had annual turnover rates of 200 percent and 15 percent in the first day. Poor treatment by employers led to labor disputes and additional turnover. Communities that tried to work with a particular group of new immigrants to help them adjust and feel at home often found they were dealing with an entirely new group of people every few months. Despite these problems, the newcomers allowed some communities to save the local school from consolidation and were thus welcomed.

The small towns in which the new immigrants found themselves were in a state of flux. Emigration of the young had been an established fact for decades and local businesses were rarely strong enough to attract young people with families. Small-town businesses, which had always sold manufactured goods trucked in from elsewhere to locals, found themselves facing competition from Wal-Mart, a larger, centralized, and more efficient version of the old general store. In the 1970s and 1980s, franchise fast-food made its appearance in the many rural towns, followed by franchise convenience stores that drove most of the mom-and-pop stores out of business. Jobs in these new retail franchises, often located in small shopping malls built on

the outskirts of regional trade centers, were cleaner, easier, and better paying. Housewives and single moms, high school kids, and college students looking for summer work found jobs there, leaving the harder tasks of fieldwork and meat cutting to immigrant and migrant labor.

The fluctuating rural and small-town population led to rates of demographic turbulence in some towns that exceeded the rate of turbulence in Minneapolis. Retirees moved to Arizona or Florida. Some became "snow-birds," driving south each year to avoid Minnesota's winters. Groups of life-long friends from one locale migrated to the same areas of Texas or Arizona and had regular picnics and outings. Such movement meant that new immigrants arrived to towns that often lacked a coherent community. While some urban scholars and activists imagined that the state's small towns were seething with racism in the face of the darker-skinned newcomers, in fact the most common reaction of rural Minnesota to these changes was no clear reaction at all. Tied ever closer to urban centers through better communications, media, and travel opportunities, much of rural Minnesota ceased to have a coherent character. Smaller towns began to look like suburban bedroom communities, feeding the larger town with workers for whom long commutes were a fair trade off for the lower housing costs that could be had in small towns.

Changes in Minnesota's population mirrored changes in its economy and politics as well. The DFL party began a slow split along what can only be described as class lines (including a heavy dose of abortion politics). Rural, blue-collar, and suburban Democrats grew disenchanted with the state party, which was increasingly run by a liberal party elite. In 1980s Governor Rudy Perpich represented the party's working-class roots and was the state's first Catholic governor and its first non-Scandinavian, non-Anglo governor in memory. Derided by critics inside and outside as "governor Goofy" for his constant stream of new ideas to promote the state and its products, the state prospered under his leadership. Although most remembered for his plan for creating a chopstick factory, most forgot that in the

Lake Minnetonka

1980s, Minnesota also became home to a growing number of high technology firms and an expanding service industry that helped shield the state from downturns in the farm economy. In 1990 party liberals jumped ship and voted for a pro-choice Republican, Arne Carlson. Carlson became the first Minnesota Republican governor to hold office for more than one term.

Neither the DFL nor the state's Republicans gained much ground with voters during the 1990s. Leaders of both parties seemed arrogant and out of touch with the concerns of state voters. In 1998, as Carlson left office, a flamboyant former pro wrestler, radio host, and suburban mayor, Jesse "the Body" Ventura upset both party candidates by winning as an Independent. Despite all the fanfare of his election, however, Ventura's time in office resembled a marketing gimmick. The state's basic policies changed but little.

⁕

Minnesota's history is inseparable from its landscapes and the mental picture the state's diverse people hold of their home state. There is little doubt that immense changes have transformed the state and its population in the past few decades, though not perhaps as much as some imagine.

Several of Minnesota's past faces have disappeared forever. The face of the land as it was before the arrival of Europeans is gone entirely. It exists now only as reconstructed by scholars or in the political mythology of those who want to imagine a time before the seemingly intractable problems of the present reared their heads. The image resembles the Biblical garden of Eden more than any reality.

Gone, too, is the heroic age of the extractive industries: the fur traders, the canoes filled with voyageurs, and the ethnically and racially mixed world they created. The logging frontier and mythology of plaid-wearing lumberjacks cutting massive stands of timber to build the cities of a growing nation are no more. Even now, the living memory of the Iron Rangers, their hard and dangerous work to draw the rich, red ore from the earth, and the mélange of ethnic cultures that made up the Range seems to be fading.

Gone, most of all, is the world of the small towns that so defined the state and its people. Its skeleton remains, dotting the highway map with a thousand names, but the values, the vitality, and the self-confidence of being at the cutting edge of a young civilization have vanished.

Yet there is much to suggest that Minnesota in the twenty-first century will not be so different from Minnesota in the last century, even if the faces and the names are new.

Minnesota is still a place of transitions. It is neither fully east nor west, neither fully Great Plains nor Great Lakes. Its south is part of the cornbelt, its north part of the north woods. Its major urban centers with their lively cultural life and economy ensure that Minnesota is never just a "fly-over" state. But it is too midwestern to be a smaller, centrally located version of San Francisco or Boston, despite the fond imagings of some.

The state is best defined by its landscape and the impression it has made on its residents: the lakes, woods, rivers, towns, and prairie. This outer geography determines an inner geography of memories that binds places to people's lives. It is not just any lake, but the lake with the family cabin. It is not just any farm on the road, but that farm where your grandparents tilled the soil. Each place in the state carries the echoes of someone's life, struggles and triumphs, sorrow and elation.

More than any event or natural feature, Minnesota is a state of simple, basic pleasures. Its history is often taken for granted by its inhabitants, but its homelike quality is what continues to make it the happy midwestern medium that its residents have so often imagined it to be.

CHRONOLOGY OF MAJOR EVENTS

BCE

10,000	End of the last Ice Age
9,500	First human presence recorded in Minnesota
6,000–5,000	Prairie Archaic Culture established in Minnesota
5,000	First copper mining around Lake Superior; first petroglyphs carved
1,000–500	Woodland Culture established in Minnesota
690	First mound building in Minnesota

CE

700	First traces of Dakota people in Minnesota
900	First agricultural production in Minnesota
1475	Ojibwe people arrive in Lake Superior region
1600	Pipestone Quarry site reaches its high point
1600–1800	Ongoing conflict between Dakota and Ojibwe
1659	Arrival of first French fur traders in MN region
1673	Jolliet-Marquette expedition reaches upper Mississippi River
1678	Sieur Du Luth claims Minnesota for France
1680	Expedition of Fr. Louis Hennepin
1680s–1700	Small French outposts temporarily established
1732	Founding of Grand Portage
1763	France loses Quebec & North American colonies
1768	Battle of Crow Wing
1780	Pembina founded
1783	Britain cedes northeast Minnesota and Wisconsin to the new United States
1787	Northwest Ordinance passed to govern new American territories
1803	Louisiana Purchase brings the remainder of Minnesota into nominal U.S. control
1805	Zebulon Pike expedition and first land treaty with Dakota
1820–1825	Construction of Fort Snelling
1836	Artist George Catlin visits Minnesota to record the lifeways of Native peoples
1837	Treaty with Ojibwe opens eastern Minnesota to logging and settlement
1840s	U.S. attempts to resettle Ho-Chunk people from Wisconsin to Minnesota
1849	Minnesota becomes an official territory of the U.S.
1851	Creation of the University of Minnesota

1851–1855	Treaties with Dakota and Ojiwbe open most of Minnesota to American settlement
1858	Minnesota achieves statehood
1861–1865	U.S. Civil War
1862–1866	U.S.–Dakota War, Dakota expelled from MN
1864	Ho-Chunk expelled from MN
1865–1900	Large scale immigration swells state's population
1866	First park established in Minneapolis
1870s	Iron ore deposits discovered in northern MN
1873–1876	Grasshopper infestation in western and southern Minnesota halts settlement
1876	Jesse James gang routed by armed citizens in Northfield after botched bank heist
1880s–1910s	Expansion of industry throughout state
1881	Small groups of Dakota return to Minnesota
1882	First iron mine opened at Tower
1885–1886	First Winter Carnival in St. Paul
1893	St. Paul-based Great Northern railroad extends from St. Paul to Seattle
1898	Battle of Sugar Point
1902	Minneapolis is America's milling capital
1917–1918	U.S. involved in World War I
1920	Lynching in Duluth of three black men shocks the state
1924	Milford mine disaster kills 42 miners
1927	Construction of Foshay Tower in Minneapolis; Lindbergh's trans-Atlantic flight
1930	Election of Floyd Olson as government marks high point of Farmer–Labor Party in Minnesota
1930–1934	Farm protests rock rural areas of the state
1934	Minneapolis Teamsters' Strike
1940s–2000s	Suburban expansion
1941–1944	American involvement in World War II
1944	Formation of Democratic Farmer–Labor Party
1945	Hubert H. Humphrey elected mayor of Minneapolis
1960	Minnesota Vikings established
1961	Washington Senators move to Minnesota and become Minnesota Twins
1964	Humphrey elected vice president of the U.S. on a ticket with President Lyndon B. Johnson
1975	First groups of "new" immigrants begin coming to Minnesota
1987	First Indian gambling casino opened in MN
1988	Twins win World Series
1991	Twins win World Series

Winter Carnival, St. Paul

1992	Mall of America opened
1998	Former pro-wrestler Jesse Ventura elected as the state's first third party candidate since 1930
2000	New professional hockey team, Minnesota Wild, debuts in St. Paul
2002	Tim Pawlenty elected governor of Minnesota

Cultural Highlights

Film

Until quite recently there were few major films that featured Minnesota in any way. Most native-born actors and filmmakers from Minnesota made their mark elsewhere. The state attempted to attract the film industry in the 1980s and 1990s with only modest success. The best-known film about the state is *Fargo,*" an offbeat comedy that poked fun at the Upper Midwest's broad Scandinavian-laced accents and its peculiar culinary inventions, such as hotdish. It met a mixed reception in the state as more than a few found it demeaning, even though Minnesotans make the same jokes about their own. ("You know you're a Minnesotan if a traffic jam is five cars stuck behind a slow tractor.")

The film *Grumpy Old Men* (1993) and its sequel *Grumpier Old Men* (1995) were the most mainstream Minnesota films. Both starred Jack Lemmon and Walter Matthau, as feuding neighbors in Wabasha, Minn., along with Ann-Margaret. The 1995 sequel added Sophia Loren. Both films did well at the box office and cemented the image of Minnesota as a land of quaint small towns filled with quirky plaid-wearing fishermen.

The state has also been featured in a variety of lesser films, from the 1972 thriller *You'll Like My Mother*, to the forgettable 1996 *Feeling Minnesota*. A variety of small independent filmmakers call the Twin Cities home, and there are many local and international film festivals throughout the year, testifying to a strong local audience. Nevertheless, the genre of *Grumpy Old Men* and its alter ego *Fargo* has proved a limited one, and filmmakers have unfortunately not found other stories to tell about the state.

LITERATURE

Minnesota has an important literary tradition, being the birthplace of F. Scott Fitzgerald and Sinclair Lewis. Fitzgerald rarely used Minnesota themes and Lewis probably used them too much, but both helped put the state on the literary map. Ole E. Rolvaag's *Giants in the Earth*, though set in the Dakotas, chronicled the hardships of Norwegian immigration and is closely related to Minnesota history. Its author taught at St. Olaf College in Northfield for many years. Vilhelm Moberg's classic four volume series *The Emigrants* described Swedish migration to Minnesota and the author is still one of the greatest writers in Swedish language.

The best-known contemporary Minnesotan writer is probably Garrison Keillor, whose *Prairie Home Companion* helped define the state's image as a place of quirky, un-hip, but commonsensical small town residents who spoke with broad Scandinavian-laced accents. His novels reinforced this theme, though as he grew more famous his work veered more into political editorializing. This "down home" Minnesotan genre was not occupied by Keillor alone, however; authors such as Bill Holm (*Boxelder Box Variations, Music of Failure*), Howard Mohr (*How to Talk Minnesotan*), and Leo Dangel (*Home from the Field*) while much less known were often closer to the lives, humor, and sorrows of ordinary rural Minnesotans.

The state has also produced a number of interesting travelogues. The best known *Canoeing with the Cree*, written in 1935 by young and then-unknown journalist named Eric Sevareid. The book recounted Sevareid's journey by canoe from Minneapolis Hudson's Bay.

Music

Most popular musicians from Minnesota made it big when they left the state—Bob Dylan being the best example. However, the state has had a significant wealth of musical talent. In the 1980s, there was even a short-lived "Minnesota sound." After Dylan, the best-known popular musician from Minnesota has been Prince Rogers Nelson, known as Prince, and for a short-lived period known simply as an unpronounceable symbol. (During the period when Prince changed his name to the unpronounceable symbol, he was commonly called the "artist formerly known as Prince" or "Symbolina.") A talented musician and promoter, Prince wrote a number of 1980s dance hits and starred in quasi-autobiographical movies such as *Purple Rain*. Prince also created a entire line of purple Prince-related merchandise: jewelry, watches, purses, scented oils, perfumes, and self-published books that he retailed through his own stores.

The Twin Cities also produced an array of punk and later alternative bands that gained some national recognition. These included The Suburbs, The Replacements, Soul Asylum, and Husker Du. The Minnesota music scene reached its zenith in 1984 when Prince, The Replacements, and Husker Du all made the top 10 of the Village Voice's critics' poll. Since then, the state has maintained a moderately successful but limited club and music scene, mainly in the Twin Cities.

Special Events
Summer

Hjemkomst Scandinavian Festival, held late June, Moorhead, Minnesota. Music, storytelling, food, and crafts highlight all Scandinavian cultures.

Bayfront Blues Festival, held mid August, Duluth, Minnesota. Showcases local and national talent playing in the city's scenic harbor.

Minnesota Bluegrass and Old-Time Music Festival, held mid August, near St. Cloud, Minnesota. The Minnesota Bluegrass & Old-Time Music Festival is the largest and most respected bluegrass event in the Upper Midwest. The Festival features a blend of national and regional professionally touring performers.

Minnesota State Fair, held last two weeks of summer, ending Labor Day, at the Fairgrounds in St. Paul. Features amusement park, exhibits, live music, and every kind of food on a stick you can imagine. One of the largest state fairs in the country.

Renaissance Festival, held August–September, near Shakopee. One of the country's largest Renaissance Festival features hundreds of costumed guests and participants reliving the Sixteenth Century.

Fall

Polish Apple Fest, second Sunday in October, Polish Museum, Winona, Minnesota. Folk dancing, museum tours, music, and apple cider and other treats highlight Winona's ethnic heritage.

Oktoberfest, held in October, New Ulm, Minnesota. German music, food, and crafts fill the streets of this historic central Minnesota town every year.

Winter

St. Paul Winter Carnival, held late January to early February, downtown St. Paul. The ice palace, parades, and treasure hunt hightlight this annual tradition where Minnesotans laugh at their proverbial winters.

Contact Information

Bloomington visitors' website with links to Mall of America:
www.bloomingtonmn.org

Duluth visitors' website: www.visitduluth.com/

Explore Minnesota Tourism
121 7th Place E
Metro Square, Suite 100
St. Paul, MN 55101
www.exploreminnesota.com

Minneapolis visitors' website: www.minneapolis.org/

Minnesota Department of Tourism
888-Tourism (868-7476)
(651) 296-5029 in the Twin Cities Area

Minnesota Historical Society
345 W. Kellog Blvd.
St. Paul, MN 55102-1906
(651) 296-6126
www.mnhs.org/places/sites/

St. Paul visitors' website: www.stpaulcvb.org/

Sources and Further Reading

General Histories & Guides

Björnson, Val. *The History of Minnesota.* 4 vols. West Palm Beach, Fla.: Lewis Historical Publishing Company, 1969.

Blegan, Theodore C. *Minnesota: A History of the State.* Minneapolis: University of Minnesota Press, 1963.

Brings, Lawrence M., ed. *Minnesota Heritage: A Panoramic Narrative of the Historical Development of the North Star State.* Minneapolis: T. S. Denison & Co., 1960.

Burnquist, Joseph A. *Minnesota and Its People.* 4 vols. Chicago: S. J. Clarke Publishing, 1924.

Castle, Henry A. *Minnesota: Its Story and Biography.* 3 vols. Chicago: Lewis Publishing, 1915.

Christianson, Theodore. *Minnesota, the Land of Sky-Tinted Waters: A History of the State and Its People.* 5 vols. Chicago: American Historical Society, 1935.

Collections of the Minnesota Historical Society, 15 vols. St. Paul: Minnesota Historical Society, 1902.

Folwell, William Watts. *A History of Minnesota.* 4 vols. St. Paul: Minnesota Historical Society, 1956.

Gilman, Rhoda R. *The Story of Minnesota's Past.* St. Paul: Minnesota Historical Society, 1989.

Larson, Paul Clifford. *Icy Pleasures: Minnesota Celebrates Winter.* Afton: Afton Historical Society Press, 1998.

Lass, William E. *Minnesota: A History,* 2nd ed. New York: W. W. Norton, 1998.

Lindquist, Maude L. and James W. Clark. *Minnesota the Story of a Great State.* New York: Charles Scribner's Sons, 1950.

Morlan, Robert. L. *Political Prairie Fire: The Non-Partisan League, 1915–1922.* St. Paul: Minnesota Historical Society Press, 1985; reprint of 1955.

Neill, Edward Duffield. *The History of Minnesota from the Earliest French Explorations to the Present Time.* Minneapolis: Minnesota Historical Society, 1882.

Szarkowski, John. *The Face of Minnesota.* Minneapolis: University of Minnesota Press, 1958.

Upham, Warren. *Minnesota in Three Centuries, 1655–1908,* 3 vols. St. Paul: Publishing Society of Minnesota, 1908.

—-. *Minnesota Place Names: A Geographical Encyclopedia,* 3rd rev. ed. St. Paul: Minnesota Historical Society, 2001.

Exploration/Territorial Era

Adams, Arthur T., ed. *The Explorations of Pierre Esprit Radisson.* Minneapolis: Ross and Haines, 1961.

Beltrami, J. C. *A Pilgrimage in America Leading to the Discovery of the Sources of the Mississippi and Bloody River; with a Description of the Whole Course of the Former, and of the Ohio.* Chicago: Quadrangle Books, 1962; reprint of 1828.

Bray, Edmund C. and Martha Coleman Bray, eds. *Joseph N. Nicollet on the Plains and Prairies: The Expeditions of 1838–39 with Journals, Letters, and Notes on the Dakota Indians.* St. Paul: Minnesota Historical Society Press, 1976.

Bray, Martha Coleman. *Joseph Nicollet and His Map.* Philadelphia: American Philosophical Society, 1994.

Callahan, Kevin L. *The Jeffers Petroglyphs: Native American Rock Art on the Midwestern Plains.* St. Paul: Prairie Smoke Press, 2001.

Carver, Jonathan. *Travels through the Interior Parts of North America in the Years 1766, 1767, and 1768,* 3rd ed. Minneapolis: Ross & Haines, 1956; reprint of 1781.

Cross, Marion E., ed. and trans. *Father Louis Hennepin's Description of Louisiana Newly Discovered to the Southwest of New France by Order of the King.* Minneapolis: University of Minnesota Press, 1938.

Gates, Charles M. *Five Fur Traders of the Northwest.* St. Paul: Minnesota Historical Society, 1965.

Goodman, Nancy and Robert. *Joseph R. Brown, Adventurer on the Minnesota Frontier, 1820–1849.* Rochester, Minn.: Lone Oak Press, 1996.

Kane, Lucile M., June D. Holmquist, and Carolyn Gilman, eds. *The Northern Expeditions of Stephen H. Long: The Journals of 1817 and 1823 and Related Documents.* St. Paul: Minnesota Historical Society Press, 1978.

Mason, Philip P., ed. *Schoolcraft's Expedition to Lake Itasca: The Discovery of the Source of the Mississippi.* Lansing: Michigan State University Press, 1958.

Parker, John, ed. *The Journals of Jonathan Carver and Related Documents, 1766–1770.* St. Paul: Minnesota Historical Society Press, 1976.

Schoolcraft, Henry. *Discovery of the Mississippi River: Summary Narrative of an Exploratory Expedition to the Sources of the Mississippi River in 1820.* Philadelphia: Lippincott, Grambo, and Co., 1855.

Where Two Worlds Meet: The Great Lakes Fur Trade. St. Paul: Minnesota Historical Society Press, 1982.

Geography and Natural/Environmental History

Amato, Anthony J., Janet Timmerman, and Joseph Amato, eds.

Draining the Great Oasis: An Environmental History of Murray County, Minnesota. Marshall: Crossings Press, 2001.

Andreas, A. T. *An Illustrated Historical Atlas of the State of Minnesota.* Chicago: n.p., 1874.

Atlas of the State of Minnesota. Fergus Falls, Minn.: Thomas O. Nelson, 1962.

Borchert, John R. and Donald P. Yaeger. *Atlas of Minnesota Resources and Settlement,* rev. ed. St. Paul: Minnesota State Planning Agency, 1969.

Hanson, John M. *Minnesota Atlas: A Sportsman Guide to Public Lands and Water Accesses.* Cambridge, Minn.: Adventure Publications, 1997.

Heinselman, Miron. *Boundary Waters Wilderness Ecosystem.* Minneapolis: University of Minnesota Press, 1996.

An Inventory of Minnesota Lakes. St. Paul: Department of Conservation, 1968.

Sims, P. K. and G. B. Morey, eds. *Geology of Minnesota: A Centennial Volume.* St. Paul: Minnesota Geological Survey, 1972.

The Vincent Atlas of Minnesota. St. Paul: St. Thomas Academy, 1985.

Water, Thomas F. *The Streams and Rivers of Minnesota.* Minneapolis: University of Minnesota Press, 1977.

ETHNIC GROUPS

Amato, Joseph A. *Servants of the Land: God, Family, and Farm, the Trinity of Belgian Economic Folkways in Southwestern Minnesota.* Marshall: Crossings Press, 1990.

Amato, Joseph A., John Radzilowski, et al. *To Call It Home: The New Immigrants of Southwestern Minnesota.* Marshall, Minn.: Crossings Press, 1996.

Anderson, Philip J. and Dag Blanck, eds. *Swedes in the Twin Cities: Immigrant Life and Minnesota's Urban Frontier.* St. Paul: Minnesota Historical Society Press, 2001.

Broker, Ignatia. *Night Flying Woman: An Ojibway Narrative.* St. Paul: Minnesota Historical Society Press, 1983.

Butcher-Younghans, Sherry. *The American Swedish Institute: A Living Heritage.* Minneapolis: American Swedish Institute, 1989.

Ebbot, Elizabeth. *Indians in Minnesota,* 4th ed. Minneapolis: University of Minnesota Press, 1985.

Feest, Christian F. and Sylvia S. Kasprycki. *People of the Twilight: European Views of Native Minnesota, 1832 to 1862.* Afton, Minn.: Afton Historical Society Press, 1999.

Glasrud, Clarence A. ed. *A Heritage Deferred: The German-Americans in Minnesota.* Moorhead, Minn.: Concordia College, 1981.

Fairbanks, Evelyn. *The Days of Rondo.* St. Paul: Minnesota

Historical Society Press, 1990.

Habenicht, Jan. *History of the Czechs in Minnesota*. St. Paul: Czechoslovak Genealogical Society, 1996; reprint and translation of 1910.

Hilger, M. Inez. *Chippewa Families: A Social Study of the White Earth Reservation, 1938*. St. Paul: Minnesota Historical Society Press, 1998; reprint of 1939.

Holmquist, June Drenning, ed. *They Chose Minnesota: A Survey of the State's Ethnic Groups*. St. Paul: Minnesota Historical Society Press, 1981.

Holt, Marilyn Irvin. *Indian Orphanages*. Lawrence: University Press of Kansas, 2001.

Ireland to Minnesota: Stories from the Heart. St. Paul: Hibernians of Minnesota, 1996.

Johnston, Patricia Condon. *Minnesota's Irish*. Afton: Johnston Publishing, 1984.

Kohl, Johann Georg. *Kitchi-Gami: Life among the Lake Superior Ojibway*. St. Paul: Minnesota Historical Society Press, 1985; reprint of 1860.

Nordstrom, Byron, ed. *The Swedes of Minnesota*. Minneapolis: T. S. Denison, 1976.

Plaut, W. Gunther. *The Jews of Minnesota: The First Seventy-Five Years*. New York: American Jewish Historical Society, 1959.

Pond, Samuel W. *The Dakota or Sioux in Minnesota as They Were in 1834*. St. Paul: Minnesota Historical Society Press, 1986.

Radzilowski, John. *Poles in Minnesota*. St. Paul: Minnesota Historical Society Press, 2005.

Rippley, La Vern J. and Robert J. Paulson. *German-Bohemians: The Quiet Immigrants*. Northfield, Minn.: St. Olaf College Press, 1995.

Scholberg, Henry. *The French Pioneers of Minnesota*. Eau Claire, Wis.: Heins Publishing, 1995.

Setterdahl, Lilly. *Minnesota Swedes: The Emigration from Trolle Ljungby to Goodhue County,* 1855–1912. East Moline, Ill.: Friends of the Emigrant Institute of Sweden, 1996.

Scott, Walter R., ed. *Minnesota's Black Community*. Minneapolis: Scott Publishing, 1976.

Spangler, Earl. *The Negro in Minnesota*. Minneapolis: T. S. Denison, 1961.

Strand, A. E., ed. *A History of the Swedish-Americans of Minnesota*. 3 vols. Chicago: Lewis Publishing Co., 1910.

Twenty Years after the Resettlement of the Vietnamese Refugees in Minnesota. Hopkins, Minn.: Vietnamese Community of Minnesota, 1997.

Valdés, Dionicio Nodín. *Barrios Norteños: St. Paul and Midwestern Mexican Communities in the Twentieth Century*. Austin:

University of Texas Press, 2000.

Vennum, Thomas. *Wild Rice and the Ojibway People.* St. Paul: Minnesota Historical Society Press, 1988.

Warren, William W. *History of the Ojibway People.* St. Paul: Minnesota Historical Society Press, 1984.

Wasastjerna, Hans R., ed. *History of the Finns in Minnesota.* Duluth: Minnesota Finnish-American Historical Society, 1957.

Zempel, Solvieg, ed. *In Their Own Words: Letters from Norwegian Immigrants.* Minneapolis: University of Minnesota Press, 1991.

Biography

Andersen, Elmer L. *A Man's Reach.* Minneapolis: University of Minnesota Press, 2000.

Berman, Edgar. *Hubert: The Triumph and Tragedy of the Humphrey I Knew.* New York: George Putnam and Sons, 1979.

Cohen, Dan. *Undefeated: The Life of Hubert H. Humphrey.* Minneapolis: Lerner Publications, 1978.

Davis, Kenneth S. *The Hero: Charles A. Lindbergh and the American Dream.* Garden City, N.Y.: Doubleday, 1959.

Flandrau, Charles E. *Encyclopedia of Biography of Minnesota.* Chicago: Century Publishing, 1900.

Gág, Wanda. *Growing Pains: Diaries and Drawings for the Years 1908–1917.* New York: Coward-McCann, 1940.

Larson, Bruce L. *Lindbergh of Minnesota: A Political Biography.* New York: Harcourt Brace Jovanovich, 1971.

Leipold, L. E. *Jeno F. Paulucci: Merchant Philanthropist.* Minneapolis: T. S. Denison,1968.

Luecke, Barbara K. and John C. Luecke. *Snelling: Minnesota's First Family.* Eagan, Minn.: Grenadier Publications, 1993.

Martin, Albro. *James J. Hill and the Opening of the Northwest.*

Local, City, and Regional Histories

Amato, Joseph A. and John Radzilowski. *Community of Strangers: Change, Turnover, Turbulence, and the Transformation of a Midwestern Country Town.* Marshall, Minn.: Crossings Press, 1999.

Amato, Joseph, and John W. Meyer. *The Decline of Rural Minnesota.* Marshall, Minn.: Crossings Press, 1993.

Anderson, David, ed. *Downtown: A History of Downtown Minneapolis and Saint Paul in the Words of the People who Lived It.* Minneapolis: Nodin Press, 2000.

Anderson, Jon L. *Two Harbors: 100 Years.* Dallas: Taylor Publishing, 1983.

Best, Joel. *Controlling Vice: Regulating Brothel Prostitution in St. Paul, 1865–1883.* Columbus: Ohio State University Press, 1998.

Carr, Florence Hart. *Roseville: A City in Search of Identity*. Roseville: n.p., 1982.

Carroll, Francis M., and Franklin R. Raiter. *The Fires of Autumn: The Cloquet-Moose Lake Disaster of 1918*. St. Paul: Minnesota Historical Society Press, 1990.

Castle, Henry. *History of St. Paul and Vicinity*. 3 vols. Chicago: Lewis Publishing, 1912.

Richard O. Davies, Joseph A. Amato, and David R. Pichaske, *A Place Called Home: Writings on the Midwestern Small Town*. St. Paul: MHS/Borealis Books, 2003.

Dominik, John J. *Three Towns into One City: A Narrative Record of Significant Factors in the Story of St. Cloud, Minnesota*. St. Cloud: St. Cloud Area Bicentennial Commission, n.d. [1976].

Dunn, James Taylor. *The St. Croix: Midwest Border River*. St. Paul: Minnesota Historical Society Press, 1979; reprint of 1965.

Glewwe, Lois A., ed. *South St. Paul Centennial, 1887–1987*. South St. Paul: Dakota County Historical Society, 1987.

Hiebert, Gareth D., ed. *Little Canada: A Voyageur's Vision*. Stillwater, Minn.: Croixside Press, 1989.

Holm, Bill. *The Heart Can Be Filled Anywhere on Earth: Minneota, Minnesota*. Minneapolis: Milkweed Editions, 1996.

Hudson, John C. *Plains Country Towns*. Minneapolis: University of Minnesota Press, 1985.

Jnes, Evan. *The Minnesota: Forgotten River*. Minneapolis: University of Minnesota Press, 2001.

Loso, Idelia. *St. Joseph: Preserving a Heritage, 1854–Present*. St. Cloud: n.p., 1989.

Maccabee, Paul. *John Dillinger Slept Here: A Crooks' Tour of Crime and Corruption in St. Paul, 1920–1936*. St. Paul: Minnesota Historical Society Press, 1995.

Millett, Larry. *Lost Twin Cities*. St. Paul: Minnesota Historical Society Press, 1992.

Nute, Grace Lee. *Rainy River Country*. St. Paul: Minnesota Historical Society, 1950.

Pichaske, David R. and Joseph A. Amato, eds. *Southwestern Minnesota: The Land and People*. Marshall, Minn.: Crossings Press, 2000.

Radzilowski, John. *Prairie Town: A History of Marshall, Minnesota, 1872–1997*. Marshall, Minn.: Lyon County Historical Society, 1997.

Raff, Willis H. *Pioneers in the Wilderness: Minnesota's Cook County, Grand Marais, and the Gunflint in the Nineteenth Century*. Grand Marais, Minn.: Cook County Historical Society, 1988.

Reardon, James Michael. *The Catholic Church in the Diocese of St. Paul from Earliest Origin to Centennial Achievement*. St. Paul: North Central Publishing, 1952.

Shutter, Marion Daniel. *History of Minneapolis: Gateway to the Northwest.* 3 vols. Chicago: S. J. Clarke Publishing, 1923.

Treuer, Robert. *Voyageur Country: A Park in the Wilderness.* Minneapolis: University of Minnesota Press, 1979.

Williams, J. Fletcher. *History of Hennepin County and the City of Minneapolis.* Minneapolis: North Star Publishing Co., 1881.

—. *A History of the City of St. Paul to 1875.* St. Paul: Minnesota Historical Society Press, 1983; reprint of 1876.

Economy, Labor, Business

Amato, Joseph A. *The Great Jerusalem Artichoke Circus: The Buying and Selling of the Rural American Dream.* Minneapolis: University of Minnesota Press, 1993.

Baerwald, Thomas John. *Minnesota Flour Milling.* St. Paul: Science Museum of Minnesota, 1979.

Larson, Arthur J. *The Development of the Minnesota Road System.* St. Paul: Minnesota Historical Society, 1966.